Rocky Mountain Trout Fishing

Rocky Mountain Trout Fishing

ML Publications
P.O. Box 1682
Wheat Ridge, CO 80034

First Edition

1 2 3 4 5 6 7 8 9

Printed in the United States of America

ISBN# 0-9617325-3-9

Merton D. Leeper
P.O. Box 1682
Wheat Ridge, Co. 80034

Designed and Typeset by:

ML Publications
P.O. Box 1682
Wheat Ridge, Co. 80034

Cover Design by:
Robert F. Wilson

I wish to dedicate this book to Chris Smith, whom I love like the son I never had and who has treated me like his father. We have shared more fishing and hunting outings in the last ten years than most people experience in a lifetime. I look forward to the good times ahead Chris . . . until then . . . Mert.

Contents

Foreword

Mert Leeper is well known throughout the United States as both an outdoor writer for several monthly's and as the author of *Colorado Trout Fishing Methods & Techniques* and *Colorado Trout Fishing — Part II. Prime Fishing Locations.* He also has to his credit six world freshwater fishing records for trout and American White Sturgeon.

The term 'Powerfishing', I think originated with Mert. He commonly fishes for 24 hours at a stretch and only quits when exhaustion or the need for food reminds him that it is time to quit. The development of his Leeper Keeper Adjusta Hook, Rocky Mountain Solunar Calendar, and the unique and novel fishing methods & techniques that he teaches at his seminars throughout the Rocky Mountains has added several new dimensions to those who follow his tips and recommendations.

Mert is one of those people who has that uncanny ability to catch unusually large fish consistently. Additionally, he is an avid archery hunter with expert ability and a marksman supreme with a rifle. Overall, his outdoor knowledge ranks among the top outdoorsmen within the Rocky Mountains. This particular book fills a void which will now allow those Rocky Mountain Anglers to know the 'Secrets of his Expertise'.

Mert Hooking & Icing a Wintertime Rocky Mountain Mackinaw

Introduction

My first memories in life related to night crawlers and trout in general. Dad taught me a few things early in life which sort of set me off into the general direction of a fishing fanatic. For instance, at five years of age, most kids were in bed sleeping at ten o'clock on Saturday nights, not me, I was in the flower garden with my very own flashlight helping Dad catch night crawlers. The other experience was my facination in learning to clean his trout . . . I begged him to save a couple for me to clean from his trips. And he always accomodated me. It was fun cutting into the stomach sack and removing the little flies, fresh water shrimp, snails, and stuff. And Dad told me that until I was an accomplished worm catcher, fish cleaner, and had the patience of Job, he wouldn't take me fishing.

I was about eight years old when I was first invited to tag along to a reservoir high in the Rocky Mountains. Since I was not really a good caster, my focus was upon how Dad impaled a night crawler or how he stacked salmon eggs upon tiny hooks. As the years flowed by and my techniques improved, each trip became a sort of contest with me, I wanted to be better than anyone I fished with and to really understand why some methods worked better than others. In high school, I had a steady girl friend, but didn't date her all of the time because I was too busy fishing.

My fishing activities represented a kind of unusual loneliness for a kid of sixteen. This was because my peers were too interested in girls and cars to ever go with me on weekend fishing trips. Well, I was interested in both of these commodities too except I had an unusual love for the out-of-doors and just couldn't get enough of it. So, I further affirmed my interest in fishing and vowed to read every bit of information on the subject that I could get my hands upon.

Today, I consider myself to be a sort of expert trout fisherman who is not expert enough to think he knows everything about this sport. It is amazing how much I seem to learn each year about Rocky Mountain Trout Fishing and the secrets of success. It is these secrets, which are all included in this publication, that I hope will make all of your fishing excursions in the Rocky Mountains complete successes.

Chapter 1

Lake Characteristics

The Life Cycle of all Lakes

Lakes come in many sizes, shapes, and depths, all share a common cycle which could take millions of years to complete or just a few decades. They begin as infertile waterways where few nutrients are present, then make a transition into a moderately fertile status.

Infertile waters (Oligotrophic) are most often thought of as those lakes found in the Canadian Shield or those Northern States which border Canada. These lakes are typically deep cold bodies of water in a setting where ice covers the surface a least seven months out of each year. Fish grow and mature slowly because of these harsh conditions. Moderately Fertile (Mesotrophic) waters can be found throughout the United States but are most often thought about when referring to areas in Southern canada or the Northern United States. These lakes most often are both deep and shallow and contain a moderate amount of nutrients to support a large variety of trout and other cold water species. The shallows of these lakes support a vast food chain which includes zoo plankton, fresh water shrimp, crayfish, etc. In this setting trout grow and mature quickly. Fertile (Eutrophic) lakes are generally found in climates characteristic to the Southern United States. You can visually locate aquatic weed beds, cattails, and water lilies in these shallow mud bottomed lakes. Dominate fish species are bass, catfish, and a large variety of sunfish and crappie.

The lakes of the Rocky Mountains are generally Oligotrophic where nutrients are scarce or Mesotrophic where an average amount of nutrients exist.

High altitude lakes (Oligotrophic) found throughout the Rocky Mountain States are generally deep cold waters where the ice cover does not usually come off until the month of June. These lakes most often contain a variety of trout species which grow slowly and rarely meet lunker proportions, this is primarily due to extreme fishing pressure, an overabundance of small trout, or most commonly a lack of nutrients to stimulate the food chain. Some of these lakes exist in a pristine setting where it is extremely difficult for all but the most hardy of men and women to traverse miles of slopes and trails to get to these gems. The trout in these lakes have had years to grow and mature into lunker proportions and to become predators to the smaller trout which has a tendency to keep these populations in control.

High altitude lakes cannot take significant amounts of fishing pressure and sustain healthy populations of trout. An example of this problem can be clearly identified when referring to the many pristine lakes found in Rocky Mountain National Park. The pressure of three million visitors a year to these lakes has altered the quality of the fishing experience because most of the larger fish have been prey to man, leaving the smaller trout to fend for themselves without predators. The net result of this type of pressure is a lake full of small fish, usually brook trout, which continue to spawn and produce new masses of small trout all competing for the limited resources of a particular lake. These problems are currently being addressed by those who manage these resources by significant increases in the creel limits where it is apparent that these conditions exist.

Moderately Fertile or Mesotrophic lakes are the predominate type of trout waters found throughout the Rocky Mountains. These waterways are really a combination of both infertile and moderately fertile waters, they characteristically have deep cool waters with numerous shallow bays and inlets which support substantial moss beds and an almost endless food supply from small celled protozoa to crayfish and schools of minnows. In these lakes, you will find rainbows, browns, brooks, cutthroats, Mackinaw, and several species of landlocked salmon.

Rivers and Streams

Rivers, streams, creeks, and springs in the Rocky Mountains all have one thing in common. The water is cool, clear, and supports the water temperature which is so critical for trout to survive and flourish. Additionally, the water is highly oxygenated year round and most stream flows fluctuate little except during the Spring runoff or those streams and rivers which have controlled rates of discharge due to the existence of dams and reservoirs upstream.

Water Phenomena

Lakes. The seasons of Spring, Summer, Fall, and Winter constitute the seasons of the calendar. In fishing terms though, there are eight seasons to consider. They are Early Summer, Mid-Summer, Fall, /Fall Turnover, Early Winter, Late Winter, Spring, and Spring Turnover. In order to really understand the characteristics of water, you must be aware that water sinks at 39.2° Fahrenheit (F) and with it oxygen that has been depleted in the depths during the seasons of Mid-Summer and Late Winter. If this phenomena did not occur, our lakes would be devoid of life and sterile.

The following diagrams will pinpoint these eight yearly angling seasons and describe where you can expect to find the trout lurking year round. But first, it is necessary to describe the ideal water temperatures of the various trout that we are seeking to place them in their proper seasonal positions. These water temperatures represent the ideal water feeding temperatures when the various trout are most active.

Rainbow Trout	**55°** **Temp. Range 44°-55°**	**Spring Spawner**
Cutthroat Trout	**55°** **Temp. Range 44°-55°**	**Spring Spawner**
Brook Trout	**54°** **Temp. Range 44°-70°**	**Fall Spawner**
Brown Trout	**60°** **Temp. Range 44°-75°**	**Fall Spawner**
Lake Trout	**50°** **Temp. Range 40°-59°**	**Fall Spawner**

There are three distinct layers of water, the epilimnion, the thermocline, and the hypolimnion. The epilimnion or upper layer is oxygen rich, whereas the hypolimnion, the lower layer can be stagnant, contain low levels of oxygen, or be devoid of oxygen. The thermocline is a layer of water between the warmer, surface zone and the colder deep water zone in a thermally stratified body of water, in which the water temperaturedecreases rapidly with depth. The water temperature and the layers of the water are directly affected by the seasons of the year.

Spring Season

The surface layer of water has just emerged from an ice on condition. It is very cool, perhaps 34°F on the surface and 39.2°F on the bottom. Water does not get any cooler than 39.2°F on the bottom of any typical infertile or moderately fertile Rocky Mountain Lake.

Early Spring

Surface ________________________________ **34°**

Oxygen rich cool layer

Epilimnion ________________________________

All trout species suspended here

Devoid of oxygen

Hypolimnion ________________________________ **39.2°**

Over the Late Winter months, the oxygen content within the depths has been depleted, forcing the trout to seek oxygenated water above the warmest place in the lake which is the bottom at 39.2°F. Now consider that the ideal water temperature of all trout listed is well above the warmest temperature in the lake and that the trout are going to congregate at the point where there is highly oxygenated water and a temperature closest to their ideal. In this example, the trout are forced to a temperature (let's say 36°F) which is cooler than the bottom (at 39.2°F) that is now devoid of oxygen into colder water with enough oxygen to support life.

Spring Turnover

Since trout will seek the water temperature closest to their ideal feeding temperature, you will find that the water temperature during this season is exactly the same from top to bottom.

Spring Turnover

Surface ________________________________ **39.2°**

Epilimnion ________________________________

Highly oxygenated surface water sinks to oxygenate the water from top to bottom. Trout are suspended from top to bottom.

Hypolimnion ________________________________ **39.2°**

As the surface warms to 39.2°F, it begins to sink, being replaced by cooler subsurface water, which is heated to 39.2°F at which time this surface water also sinks taking with it highly oxygenated water to the depths. The trout are disbursed from top to bottom.

Early Summer

Three distinct layers of water are now forming and the water continues to be richly oxygenated from top to bottom.

Early Summer

Surface ______________________________ **65°**

Epilimnion **Highly oxygenated**

______________ **Browns 60°**

______ **Cutthroat & Rainbow 55°**

____

Thermocline **Highly oxygenated**

______________ **Brook 54°**

____

Hypolimnion **Highly oxygenated**

____________ **Mackinaw 50°**

______________________________ **39.2°**

Understanding water phenomena, temperature impacts on the water, and fish movement will allow you to better estimate where the fish are during any season. In the balmy warm months of the year, you can now clearly understand why the fish surface in the evening and morning hours. It is likely, in any Rocky Mountain lake, that as the evening hours cool, sometime after dark, the brown trout will become extremely active on the surface (which has cooled to their 60°F ideal water temperature). Likewise, as the waters continue to cool throughout the night and early morning hours, the rainbow and cutthroat trout become active and hit the surface which has cooled to their 55°F ideal feeding temperature.

You will note that I stated that brown trout are principally noctournal and feed during the cycle of their ideal water temperatures which is usually at night. In the morning hours, the brown trout do not usually have an opportunity to enjoy another feeding frenzy because once the sun hits the surface of the water, it quickly warms up to a temperature beyond the 60° level. This is usually mid-morning when the sun is bearing down upon the water and the rainbows and cutthroats have ceased their feeding activity.

Mid-Summer

In Mid-Summer, the trout are most active in the thermocline layer where their ideal water temperatures generally exist. Mackinaw or lake trout are suspended in the uppers layers of the hypolimnion or lower layers of the thermocline.

Mid-Summer

Surface ———————————— **70°**

Highly oxygenated but warm

Epilimnion

————————————

Oxygenated cold temps

Thermocline

Brown 60°
Cutthroat & Rainbow 55°
Brook 54°
Mackinaw 50°

————————————

Oxygen only in upper portion of this layer

Hypolimnion

———————————— **39.2°**

Late summer further forces these fish upward to higher temperatures than are ideal because the hypolimnion layer has become stagnant and little oxygen is left.

Early Fall

Continued fair weather, comparable to late Summer, further depleates the oxygen content of the water in both the hypolimnion layer and the lowest portion of the thermocline.

Early Fall

Surface ______________________________ **68°**

Epilimnion

Highly oxygenated-Still Warm

Brown 60°

____

Upper level-oxygenated & cold

Cutthroat & Rainbow 55°

Thermocline

Brook 54°

Mackinaw 52°

______________________________ 50°

Hypolimnion

Stagnant & devoid of oxygen

______________________________ 39.2°

Note that the Mackinaw trout is forced out of the hypolimnion layer because it cannot support life.

Fall Turnover

As the cool breezes and temperatures of Winter approach, the surface water cools down to 39.2°F. At 39.2°F water sinks. As it sinks, it takes with it the highly oxygenated surface water to the bottom. The subsurface warmer layers of water then replace the surface water, which is then cooled to 39.2°F and it sinks to the bottom. This process continues until both the epilimnion and hypolimnion layers of water are oxygen rich. Eventually, the water from top to bottom is 39.2°F. The thermocline layer of water at this time ceases to exist.

Fall Turnover

Surface	**39.2°**
	Rainbow
Epilimnion	**Mackinaw**
	Brook

Warmer surface layers of water replace the sinking surface water.

Hypolimnion	
	Brown
	Cutthroat
	39.2°

To the trout fisherman, this is the time of the year that all trout species can be caught from the surface waters to the bottom. Before the completion of the Fall Turnover, the fish are especially active, this is because the subsurface water temperature is variable as the sinking surface water mixes with it. Eventually, as Early Winter approaches, the water is 39.2°F from top to bottom and the trout become sluggish and lethargic because they are existing at temperatures below their ideal.

Early Winter

Artic Storms and sub-zero temperatures have created substantial surface ice. The freezing upper layers of water have forced the trout into the warmer oxygenated (from the Fall Turnover) bottom water, which is now the warmest place in the lake at 39.2°F.

Early Winter

Surface Ice	______	**30°**
	Oxygen rich but very cold	
Epilimnion		
	______	**36°**
Hypolimnion		
	Warmer temperatures & oxygen rich from Fall Turnover. All trout are in this layer.	
	______	**39.2°**

As Late Winter approaches, the oxygen in the lower layer begins to deteriorate and forces the trout into the cooler upper layers. If the oxygen completely deteriorates in a lake, the result is winter kill.

Late Winter

Note that Early Winter and Late Winter trout fishing are as different as night and day, and that in the Early Winter all trout fishing activity is on the warm 39.2°F bottom. Late Winter trout fishing activity is primarily limited to suspended trout. This is because the lowest layer of water is devoid of oxygen and cannot support fish life.

Late Winter

Surface Ice	______	**30°**
	Oxygen exists but very cold	
Epilimnion		
	All trout in this layer	
	______	**36°**
Hypolimnion		
	Devoid of oxygen	
	______	**39.2°**

A Typical Mesotrophic Lake nestled High in the Rocky Mountains.

Weather & Mooncycles can make or break a day of trout fishing.

Chapter 2

Moon Cycles & Weather Conditions

The aura of a full moon casts an erie glow upon the landscape, creating mystic shadows which seem to move about and create phantoms in our minds. Caution is the rule for animals during the cycle of the Full Moon. It is because their natural predators are nocturnal. Trout also react in strange ways during the cycles of the Moon.

I have often wondered how many people are aware of the effects the Moon has upon the Earth, especially the tidal action upon the seas, the movement of the Earth's crust and the effects upon inland lakes. Trout may be the most sensitive of all cold water fish to lunar activities.

For instance, trout rarely feed during the cycle of the Full Moon. All lakes are affected from the small impoundments to the large reservoirs. The impact of a Full Moon can be measured by increased gravitational pulls which are most apparent upon the seas where tidal activity fluctuates several feet per day. The Earth's crust also feels this gravitational action on all land and water surfaces. Trout fishing in the Rocky Mountains is best during the cycle of the Dark of the Moon.

This explanation of the cycles of the Moon is not intended to be scientific in orientation but its concepts work year after year and decade after decade. The light of the Moon also has a dramatic effect upon the predators in the water, from the smallest nymph to the feeding minnows and subsequent larger trout. In the darkness predators feed upon predators, much like a 'mug' in a dark alley sneaking up to rob his victim. In moonlight, these predators of the food chain are wary and unusually cautious, thus, the trout bite is interrupted until the light disappears over the mountains.

To explain in more detail — the Moon has four cycles which change every 29 to 30 days. These cycles are usually listed on calendars as the New Moon, First Quarter, Full Moon, and Last Quarter.

The best fishing for trout happens during the New Moon or the Dark of the Moon. At this time, the gravitational activity upon the inland lakes and river systems is at its lowest level. Trout tend to lose their caution and go on feeding binges when no Moon is visible. As the cycles progress from the New Moon (Dark of the Moon) to the First Quarter and the subsequent Full Moon, the fishing tails off to mediocrity or worse. As the Last Quarter peaks, it is time to plan your fishing trip. The best fishing is four days prior and up to the date of the New Moon.

You may have noticed my terminology when discussing the New Moon, I refer to it as the Dark of the Moon. If you analyze the Moon cycles, you will find that some years there will be thirteen Full Moons, while in other years there will be thirteen New Moons or Dark of the Moons. These conditions are present when two Full Moons or two Dark of the Moons happen within the same month. The second Full Moon within a single month is known as a Blue Moon, while the second Dark of the Moon in a single month is known to produce some fabulous trout activity.

I have often been asked whether this explanation relates to night fishing only. The answer is no. Fishing by the rise and fall of the Moon is relevant day or night. Remember that in your local newspaper, you will find specific information on when the Moon rises and sets. In the daytime, you may not be able to see the Moon because of the light of the Sun but you can be assured it is there. For instance, have you ever fished in the early morning hours when the fishing just turned off when it should have been good and then you checked the paper for the time of the morning Moonrise and found it was 9:00 a.m. — which was just about the time the fishing turned off. Thus, this method is equally effective both day and night.

With the cycles described and the knowledge of when the best trout fishing exists, it is possible to cheat a little and gain even more days or portions of days when fishing will be excellent. Simply check your local newspaper where the weather reports are given and you will find the exact times of the Moonrise and Moonset. Add one and one half hours, for the Moonrise and subtract off of the Moonset time one and one half hours. This adjustment is necessary because of the high Rocky Mountains. If you are fishing on the flats, then this adjustment is not necessary. This information will allow you to plan the hours you wish to fish.

For instance, if the Moon rises at 9:00 a.m., fish until 10:30 a.m. (even though you may not be able to see the Moon in the daylight, it is present) or if fishing at night and the Moonset is at midnight, then the best fishing will begin at 10:30 p.m. when the Moon falls below the high mountain ranges.

We have discussed water phenomena, ideal feeding temperatures and Moon cycles at length but we are still missing a valuable component to complete the picture which represents the best all around conditions to fish for trout. This component relates to the weather. Again, the explanation relating to weather phenomena and how it relates to a great trout fishing experience is not scientific but is based on forty years of fishing principles that have proven time and time again that trout are sensitive to weather conditions.

For years, I thought that a rising barometer and fair weather conditions coupled with the right Moon and water temperatures meant outstanding trout fishing. Unfortunately, this combination did not always work, in fact, I clearly remember time and time again how good the trout fishing is just before a storm and how equally bad it is just after it passes.

What happened was this. The barometric pressure was high several hours before the storm, signaling an area of high pressure or fair weather conditions. As the storm built and swept over the mountains, the barometer began to drop or create an area of low pressure — which is an indication of stormy or overcast weather. It took a few hours for this condition to develop, meanwhile, the trout became more and more active until a feeding frenzy took place a few minutes before the storm hit.

The rule of thumb is to fish for trout when the barometric pressure is lower than the average high. Or better described, fish when clouds are present in the mountains. You will find that most of the time in the late afternoon it clouds up in the mountainous areas and you can even see rain falling. But more often than not, the storm passes clear of the water your fishing and you enjoy the benefits of this low barometer by creeling a number of very active feeding trout.

This explanation can be further expanded into two controversial schools of thought . . . the lateral line vs the swim bladder. The lateral line is a faint line which runs along the middle of each side of the trout, it is composed of cells which allow trout to sense vibrations in the water which could relate to the presence of larger predators or a food source such as a small school of minnows nearby. The swim bladder is an internal organ which allows fish to suspend itself at any level throughout the depths.

With these definitions in mind it is easy to ponder whether the barometric pressure affects the lateral line or the swim bladder or both. I suspect it affects the sensitive internal swim bladder and turns off the feeding mechanism.

Another tip, which you can count on when fishing for trout is to fish with the wind blowing in your face. It is a well documented fact that trout assault the shallows under these conditions and feed heavily on the displaced fresh water shrimp, nymphs, insects, and drowning flying insects washed about by the action of the wind and waves.

To close this chapter I wish to provide you with some Summertime reflections which will provide you with information that compliments Chapter 1 concepts and adds to the information thus far covered in this Chapter.

Each year for the last several years, I have conscientiously kept logs which relate to the numbers of trout each outing. The last five years all have one commonality, in that, the month of August has really been the pits for fishing large impoundments even though all other factors appeared to be favorable. For instance, a favorable Moon, falling barometer, and surface temperature equal to the ideal feeding temperatures of trout have often resulted in some very disappointing August fishing ventures.

August is typically very hot in the mountains and is the transitional month between the seasons of Summer and Fall in the Rocky Mountains. Early August is hot as blazes, while the last few days of this month see the temperatures losing just a few degrees each week thereafter into the first two weeks of September when it is distinctly cooler. Are trout sensitive to these weather conditions and why?

Early August surface temperatures often reach 70° by ten o'clock in the morning and continue to heat the upper surface layers of this water until Sunset. These conditions ideally foster substantial algae and zoo plankton growth early in the month to literal explosions of growth so heavy that it is clearly visible to the eye on both the surface and subsurface. Additionally, at this time of year, the lower layers of the water have become stagnant and have lost enough oxygen to force the trout into the upper algae filled layers. Subsurface moss growth also contributes to an oxygen loss in the depths which will force the trout into the more highly oxygenated warmer surface layers of the water.

These factors create two situations, which in combination result in less than desirable fishing results. Heavy algae and large colonies of zoo plankton have created what appears to be an endless food supply of gourmet food for the trout. To them this layer is comparable to humans nibbling on small salad shrimp, cashew peanuts, or smoked salmon. At this time of year it is common to locate huge schools of trout and salmon suspended just a few feet below the surface at the upper edge of the cool Thermocline layer and the lower edge of the Epilimnion layer. These fish are literally gorging themselves and totally ignoring anglers offerings which they must pursue and expend energy. As the month progresses, significant moss and vegetation growths add to the lower level oxygen depleation problems forcing the trout into the upper layers of water which are just a few degrees above their normal active feeding levels. This results in trout which are lethargic, somewhat stressed, and inactive. Thus, an endless gourmet food supply and conditions in which trout must suspend in warmer than their ideal (but, I might add a safe temperature for survival) equates into the Summer doldrums.

The way to get around this problem is to fish the highly oxygenated inlets where the water is cool and the trout are active or to fish the excellent river systems associated with the Rocky Mountains. Note that the Summer doldrums end with sustained cool weather and the Fall Turnover which re-oxygenates these fisheries from top to bottom.

Twin Rocky Mountain Rainbows caught by Bob Fisher.

Chapter 3

Bait Fishing

Bait fishing is probably the oldest and most successful method of taking trout consistently. Sounds simple . . . just take a worm, slap it on a hook, wing it out, and wait for a strike.

There is much to say about bait fishing. Selection of bait, rigging techniques, and presentation are the keys to success beyond your wildest expectations. This chapter will detail the art of baitfishing both in lakes and river systems. You will, in some cases, find some very unique, novel, and unusual techniques which will dispel many of your old fishing habits and replace them with new tested methods based on years of research.

In most of the Rocky Mountain States there are restrictions in the use of live minnows in trout waters. This is due to the possibility that a new undesirable species could thrive in a trout lake and upset the ecological balance. Thus, the use of dead minnows is a common practice, but why do some varieties work better than others?

It is quite common to read a variety of trout fishing articles that discuss the use of ciscos (common in waters of the Northeastern U.S.) or other specific types of shiners, chubs, and shad, then to attempt to use them in the waters of the Rocky Mountains. In most bait shops you will find a wide variety of jarred minnows or frozen whole fish which originate outside of the Rocky Mountain Area. It is best to buy or seine your own local live baits to assure freshness and the use of a minnow that is indigenous to your locality.

The use of whole dead or fileted suckers, skulpins, chubs, and shiners will fill your stringer to the brim with larger and less wary trout. The specific methods of rigging and technique are as follows (remember that in most of the Rocky Mountain States, you may not transport live minnows, so you must allow them to die first).

Suckers

In waters where you can expect to catch Mackinaw (Lake Trout), rig a whole sucker of six to eight inches in length using the Leeper Keeper Adjusta-Hook described in the Knots and Rigging Chapter and attach as follows:

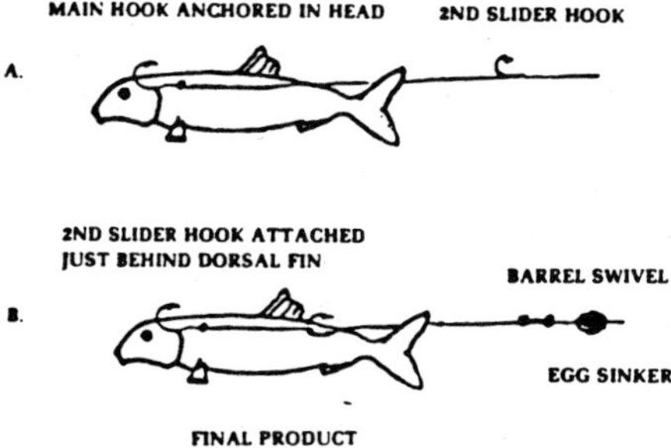

To fish this rig it is important to use an open faced reel and sturdy rod which will cast this rig far from the bank or your boat. Note that in the following illustration, intended for ice fishing, you use no sinkers that are visible on your line . . . open water fishermen use a barrel swivel/egg sinker combination to achieve maximum casting distance.

Note that in winter, the sinker goes into the suckers gullet and is allowed to sink to the depths on its own through an ice hole.

Once your rig has sunk to the bottom, keep your bail or free spool open and place a styrofoam peanut (packing material) onto your monofilament line just below your first eyelet and wait for quality action. Your first indication of a strike will be that the peanut has moved, it could be just a few inches or as much as twenty yards. It is time to be aware that you have a strike, but *do not attempt to set the hook,* these fish are simply picking up the bait and taking it away in their jaws, much like a Northern Pike does.

It is common knowledge that trout have a tendency to school, the smaller the fish, the larger the school. Or the larger the fish, the smaller the school. Thus, on this first run, your lunker is simply grabbing your bait and taking it away from the others to a place where the feasting can be done in private.

After this first run, place another peanut below your rod tip. When the second run begins, it is time to get excited because your trout has swallowed the bait and will begin taking your line out at an alarming rate. Hit hard at this time and expect a Mackinaw of immense proportions to be your catch.

Another successful method to trick these denizens of the deep (if you have a boat) is to set up with the Leeper Keeper Adjusta-Hook and drift fish. Your depth finder will do the locating, all you have to do is raise or lower your bait to the fish.

MINNOWS

The use of dead minnows as a trout bait has not really caught on in the Rocky Mountains. This is probably because of their lack of availability or the trouble of buying them alive, having to kill them, and then transporting them on ice and the convenience of picking up long lasting prepared baits (such as Berkley Power Bait, salmon eggs, marshmallows, cheese baits) or live night crawlers. Jarred minnows are not a common sight in most bait shops in the Rocky Mountains, but when they are available they are most effective. Fresh is best, but jarred is second best.

Select a minnow of about two to three inches in length, place it aside while you thread a needle (larger than the minnow) through your monofilament, then carefully push the needle through the head, body cavity, and out the vent. At this point, disconnect the needle, clip a couple of inches of monofilament off and attach a hook to your line using a Trilene knot.

Once your minnow is rigged, it is necessary to get into your tackle box and find your syringe (to blow up night-crawlers) and put air into the minnows back. This creates buoyancy and the appearance of a wounded minnow.

Example:

Two methods of presentation work well. The first, which is primarily a river application, is to attach a split shot about eighteen inches up the line, then cast into the ripples, just above the pools. If the minnow actually reaches the depths of the pools without a strike, then slowly pull the minnow toward you stopping every two to three feet. This method also works well in lakes just off shallow rocky edges adjacent to weedbeds.

The most effective lake presentation is to attach a clear plastic float (bubble) four feet above the minnow with a very small split shot positioned eighteen inches above the minnow. Cast out as far as you can into an area in which you can visualize weed beds or moss and an apparent drop off, retrieve very slowly, stopping every couple of feet. Your strikes should be bone jarring.

Another modification of this method for lake applications is to attach an Adjusta Bubble, fill it completely full of water, cast it out into deep water and retrieve in the same manner as previously described. The bubble will sink a few feet below the surface upon retrieval and the minnow will appear as if it is a live wounded bait fish.

Legal Live Baits

The most traditional and available live baits of all are earthworms and nightcrawlers, closely followed by grubs, larvae, and hoppers. Lesser known but equally effective trout baits include waterdogs (aquatic gilled stage of the salamander), hellgrammites (Western Stone Fly nymph, crickets, and crayfish.

Hellgrammites

In the Eastern United States most of the rivers contain the true hellgrammite which is known as the "carnivorous, dark brown, aquatic larva of the Dobson Fly." In the Rocky Mountains, the term hellgrammite refers to the "two inch, dark brown nymph of the Stone Fly family." The Western hellgrammite is not nearly as difficult to use because it will not attack you with its sharp jaws like its cousin will. The Western variety is ugly and crawly, but will not hurt you and is easy to get. This bait is the bait of choice when river fishing throughout the Rocky Mountains.

The technique is to find a rocky bottomed river, wade out a few feet, put your net down river from yourself (the net should have a fine screen inserted — nylon and cheese cloth work well), and to simply displace rocks with your feet. You will be surprised to find that in ten to fifteen minutes you will have collected a couple of hundred of these one to three inch creatures. I usually keep the big ones and throw back the small ones. They cannot bite, so be brave, grab one and put it on a hook. This is the most natural river bait you can use.

Attach this bait by placing the hook just under the collar behind the head. Fish in the ripples, just before they give way to pools. Fishing the inlet to lakes in this manner is also effective. Use a small split shot a couple feet above your hook to keep the bait down.

Crayfish

Crayfish are present in most Rocky Mountain lakes and river systems. Their use by trout fishermen is practically nil. This is probably due to the fact that they are not generally through of as a trout bait.

Mackinaw, rainbows, and brown trout are especially fond of them in the two to four inch length range. Attach the crayfish to a sliding sinker rig (as shown in b. page 22), cast out into the depths, wait five or ten minutes, then lift your rod tip and pull your line about six feet closer and repeat. In rivers, crayfish need to be rigged with the use of a three way swivel. Presentation relates to a cast upstream to about sixty degrees, allow the bait to cascade into or around deep rocks and then to a pool. If you do not get a strike once your crayfish is in the pool, wait for a while, and then retrieve only a few feet at a time. This type of retrieve usually results in a strike.

Salamanders

Often called mudpuppies or waterdogs, the aquatic gilled salamander is only a stage in the life of a land creature. In this aquatic stage, salamanders will definitely yield to you a trout of such great proportions that you will surely place it on your mantle.

Salamander use is generally limited to lake applications. Using the Leeper Keeper Adjusta-Hook, attach the terminal hook through the lips and the slider hook into the tail, then attach a large red and white bobber about six to eight feet above your 'dog'.

Presentation is the key to success. You must read the

water to be certain that your 'puppy' is in a deep channel, on the edge of a drop off when using a boat, or from a steep shoreline. Cast as far out as you can and watch the action. Your 'dog' will work the bobber continuously trying to seek the solace of the mud bottom below.

Another tip in which success is measured in pounds is to use this same method at night during the phase of the Dark of the Moon or New Moon. Use one of the new floats which sport a small red light powered with a lithium battery. This way you can see the strike (a red light does not deter a trout from striking). A large salamander, eight to ten feet under the surface at night, is just to much for a large trout to resist.

Salamanders are generally available from those bait shops who cater to warm water fishing enthusiasts. Channel catfish, walleye, largemouth bass, and northern pike all keep 'waterpuppies' high on their list of preferred foods.

Grasshoppers and Crickets

These baits are primarily used in river systems where they are a natural part of the ecosystem. It is very common to see trout rising for grasshoppers and crickets washed into the river by wind or rain. Fishermen all know the merits of using these baits but sometimes expend so much energy trying to run them down or play 'bomber' with large rocks (which keeps them from flying but mangles them beyond practical use as a bait) that they give up chasing them.

Here are two easy methods to catch both these insects. For catching grasshoppers effortlessly always have along in your vehicle an old fuzzy wool blanket. Have you and a friend grasp the ends and slowly run through the weeds and 'viola', you instantly have several dozen grasshoppers attached to your blanket by their barbed hind legs and they are not the least bit damaged.

Fishing grasshoppers is most effective when using a fly rod/reel in combination with a floating fly line. Cast across the ripples and expect a hit just as the bait falls behind a large boulder, an undercut bank, or just as it glides into the pool below the ripple. Attach the hopper just under its collar behind the head.

Crickets seem to be used very little by trout fishermen because of the difficulty of gathering enough to make it worthwhile. Here is a trick which will allow you to collect as many as you desire. Go down to your nearest supermarket and purchase some french bread. Cut the loaf in half. With one half make sandwiches and the other hollow out with your hand or a large spoon. Place the non-sandwich half in a moist weed field, preferably near an irrigation ditch, and leave overnight. In the morning, you will find a generous supply of crickets inside your bread trap, simply cap off your bread and head to your nearest stream. And if all else fails and your lost on the river and starved, you can always empty out the crickets and eat the french bread!

Fish crickets in the same manner as you would hoppers.

Mice

Small field mice are common casualties of severe rain storms and carelessness around riverbeds and inlets to lakes. It is amazing how comfortably they swim through water.

Several years ago, while fishing in one of the large Rocky Mountain River Systems, I hooked and landed a large brown trout which was full of an assortment of baits, including two small field mice. Since this experience, I have experimented with small mice as trout bait and found the results most pleasing. The best fishing with mice is during the hot months and at night.

The secret to catching large trout on mice is to first make a state-of-the-art harness in which the hook does not even pierce the mouse. Take a piece of velcro (less than one-half inch in diameter) and of about four inches in length (this tab is for the hook to be fastened into). Then place this harness around the mouse and be sure the velcro tab is on the mouses stomach side. Then attach the hook between your tab and the harness.

This rig will not harm the mouse or allow it to escape if

attached firmly. The best presentation is to float the mouse into a current swift enough to cascade it into a deep pool. Lake applications require the use of a boat or the ability to gently float this quarry into a deep inlet where the current flows with gusto so that the mouse is carried deep into the lake channel. Boat anglers can simply release their casting mechanism and motor away twenty five yards or so and allow the mouse to swim all over the place. At night, the mouse will not last long —carnivorous brown trout will attack it at will.

Larvae

There are two forms of larvae — aquatic and terrestrial.

Aquatic larvae are known as nymphs and live their first several months or years of life underwater. As they mature, this waterborne insects molts (sheds its skin) several times until, at last, the full grown larvae seeks the solace of the surface to emerge into a dun or immature adult insect. In 24 to 48 hours, the dun usually develops into an adult insect, its sole purpose is to find a mate, breed, and fertilize or lay eggs. These eggs are laid either on the water surface where they cascade down into the depths or on a surface above the water where they fall into the water and sink to the bottom renewing the cycle of life.

These insects are winged. Examples include the Mayfly, Stonefly, Mosquitoes, Dragonflies, Damselflies, etc.

Terrestrial Larvae. This type of larvae live out their entire life cycle on the land. They characteristically develop from eggs into a larvae stage and most often develop into a pupal or cocoon stage before emerging as adult insects.

Beetles, caterpillars, flies and wasps are examples of terrestrial. Their larvae include mealworms (Darkling Beatles);, Wasps (Euro-larvae — these eggs are commercially dyed into the colors of red, white and blue); waxworms (Bee Moths); Maggots such as Mousees and Silver Wigglers (flies); Grubs (June Bugs) and thousands of others of which only an 'insectologist' could list.

It is interesting to note that most larvae sold in bait shops are the readily accessible land born varieties and not the aquatic born variety. We have heard over and over from flyfishermen, 'match the hatch'. Now the bait fishermen have a motto too, 'match the larvae'. This is of the utmost importance if your fishing a river or lake and emerging stonefly nymphs are making their last transition from nymph to adulthood by swimming from the safety of the river or lake bottom to the surface. The section on hellgrammites describes how to collect these nymphs and their use as a bait.

Upon completion of the breeding season for the nymphs (usually May through August), a transition can be made to the easily propagated land larvae for the rest of the season. Land larvae, such as mealworms are excellent for use in the early Spring and through the ice in Winter.

Worms

There are many types, sizes, and varieties of worms. For our purposes though, the focus will be on worms in general and the grandaddy of them all, the night crawler. All worms have some very interesting traits, such as: both have male and female organs but cannot fertilize themselves; they have a head and tail, the head is the end where the band encircles the body. This band is also the fertilization center where the eggs develop; and worms can regenerate new heads and tails when they are severed.

Rigging

There is a small controversy among bait fishermen regarding the various ways to rig up for trout. The two most common are to either place your weight (A) about two feet above your line or to place it on the terminal end of the line (B).

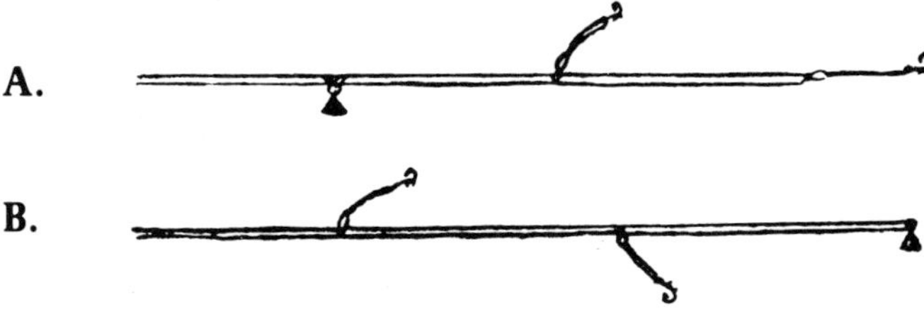

There are some advantages to both. In (B), when fishing fairly deep water full of vegetation, the sinker is grounded on the bottom allowing the bait to rest above the vegetation. In (A), the bait is presented first and rests directly on the bottom awaiting a big fat trout to come along. The best method is (C), where a swivel without a snap and a swivel with a snap is used in conjunction with a bell weight, leader and appropriate hooks. It looks like this:

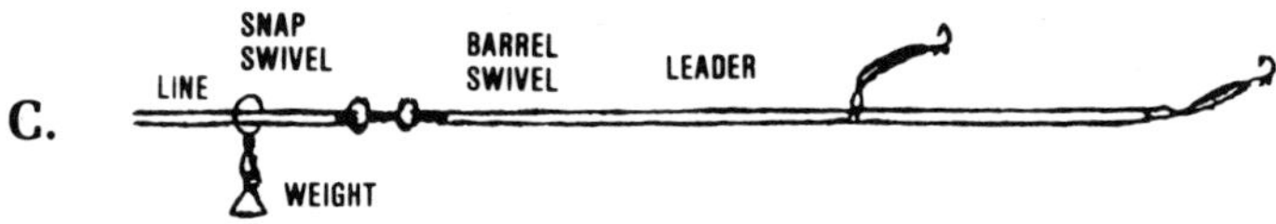

This method is the best an unfortunately is the most time consuming to prepare. This setup allows the line to freewheel through the swivel and thus when a strike occurs there is little or no drag. If your are fishing for lake trout, this setup makes the difference between catching and losing a wary lunker.

When using nightcrawlers, the point of the hook always goes through the end of the crawler up to the first barb, then loop the crawler and impale it again up to the end of the hook leaving two or three inches to crawl around.

In lakes where there is an abundance of vegetation, an effective method of using nightcrawlers is to make them float off the bottom with a method C rig. This procedure requires a syringe (purchased at any drugstore or tackle shop) and a knowledge of which is the head and tail sections of the crawler. Remember that the head end is the end with the band around it. This method is as follows:

Pull the plunger back on the syringe, fill it full of air, then inject the crawler at or near the band, under their skin, but not through to the innards. The crawler will blow up like a balloon.

Cast this bait out and the crawler will not only float off the bottom, out of the moss, but will wiggle its tail profusely attracting any trout within range.

Another excellent method used to present the crawler as naturally as possible is to thread it internally onto your hook. You need a mini piece of hollow copper tubing and a section of an Aspen branch for a handle. Drill a hole into the Aspen handle, insert the tubing, and you have made a worm threader. It is used as follows:

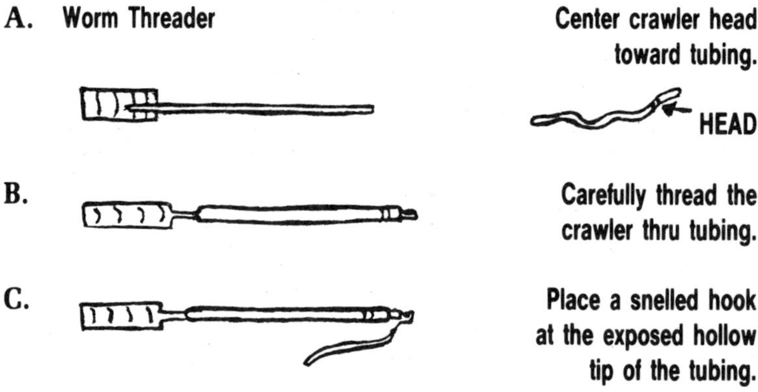

D. 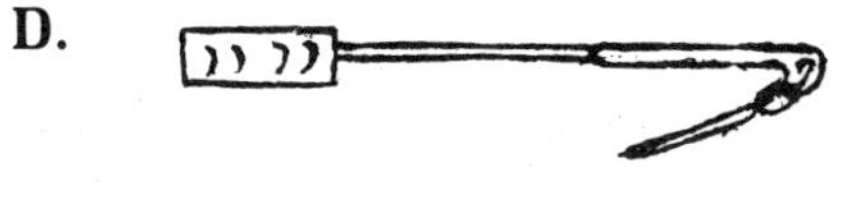

Push crawler onto hook. Hook is completely hidden and crawler does not seem damaged.

E. 

Final product

This is an especially effective way to rig crawlers for fishing streams or when trolling.

Manufactured Baits

Salmon Eggs

In order to use salmon or trout eggs they must be properly preserved or processed. The process is simple, but unless you do this all of the time, it is probably not worth your effort. I would recommend that you purchase single eggs in jars. You will notice that the commercial purchased eggs in jars seem to be larger than trout eggs. This is generally the case because commercial eggs actually come from large coastal salmon.

The preparation and use of seasonal spawn bags is another matter. This spawn is available in the Spring from rainbow and cutthroats and from brown, brook, Kokanee salmon, and lake trout in the fall. The process is as follows:

A. Remove egg sacks from fish, rinse, and drain well.

B. Leave on ice or refrigerated for a couple of days.

C. Cut the sacks or egg skeins into pieces that will accommodate the hooks you intend to use for this purpose.

D. Roll these egg clusters into a solution of Borax (which is a preservative).

E. Refrigerate if you are going to use the clusters in the immediate future or freeze them if usage is down the road.

I generally do not take the time to process clustered eggs but instead use commercial bottled salmon eggs and cluster them on a size ten or twelve barbed hook. The goal is to cluster at least four or five. In lakes, the cluster method is extremely effective but in rivers a single egg gets the nod. This is probably due to the strong currents of rivers which tend to naturally wash single eggs about after natural spawning.

Another very successful egg bait is called Strawberry Shortcake. This bait requires a marshmallow sanwiched between two eggs on a hook, one above and one below. I have seen this bait work when all others failed.

For egg applications, rig as you would for river bait or lake applications.

Cheese

Velveeta cheese has always been a good trout bait. It can be molded to look like natural eggs and when wet, it emulates a milky white substance similar to natural eggs. Thus, it is an attractant and a bait that trout take readily.

Marshmallows

Why trout like marshmallows has always been a mystery to me but, never-the-less, they are effective. Garlic salmon colored mini-marshmallows coated with crushed cheese crackers work well. The formula is as follows:

A. Purchase one bag of mini-marshmallows (white), a clove of garlic, garlic oil, a salmon colored food coloring, and cheese crackers.

B. Mash the clove of garlic and place into the bottom of a quart canning jar. Place a couple of napkins over the garlic.

C. Mash cheese crackers.

D. While dyeing the marshmallows mix in mashed cheese crackers to create a coating.

E. Before placing this creation into the jar, first sprinkle a small amount of garlic oil onto the edges of the napkins. Then place dyed 'mallows' into jar and seal.

Change marshmallows regularly when using them as a bait, the water has a tendency to dissolve them.

Cut Bait

In many large lakes and reservoirs throughout the Rocky Mountains, the recommended bait of choice for brown and Mackinaw is either strips of sucker meat or filets. There is no secret to the process, when using a whole filet, cut off the filet beginning at the dorsal fin to the tail (one side at a time). Be sure not to scale the fish . . . precious fish oils trapped under these scales will act as an attractant. Use a Leeper Keeper Adjusta-Hook to attach two hooks into the filet.

When using strips, cut wedges approximately three inches long and one inch wide. The key to effectively using this bait is to notch the tail or cut the tail to form two flaps of filet. This significantly improves the action. Strips are effective utilizing jigging methods.

Trout Surfacing for a Spring May Fly Hatch.

Chapter 4

Flyfishing

The use of a flyrod, flyreel, and line by the general angler is often seen as difficult and appropriate only for the expert angler. It should be noted that this method is only one of many that the all around trout angler needs to understand and utilize.

It is interesting to note that modern fly tackle combined with stream/lake basics on 'how to use a flyrod, reel and line' will take you virtually from no practical application of flyfishing to about sixty percent efficiency overnight. The additional forty percent success factor relates to a knowledge of patterns, their use, and some unique and novel applications of presentations and retrieves discussed throughout this chapter.

I will never forget my first experience in purchasing a fly rig (over thirty years ago). My uncle, who knew I was so interested in all types of trout fishing decided to provide the funds to purchase a bamboo flyrod . . . Upon receipt of the funds, I conned John, my neighbor, into trading me his father's brand new flyrod which was still in the case and for only two pocket knives (Keen-Cutters) and a box of 22 long rifle shells. What I didn't know was that his father had zillions of these flyrods in which he purchased overseas and gave them away as Christmas gifts to business clients and associates.

In any event, I had my rod and enough cash to obtain a

reel and the necessary line to complete this rig. Two days later, my dad, took me fishing on the Colorado River in Colorado. He used lures and bait, while I tried my new flyrod and associated equipment.

To say that I had problems was the understatement of the century. I could not cast well, retrieve properly, or present my fly in such a way as to even catch a minnow. Thus, I quickly changed to my trusty spinning rod and did not use or see the likes of this rig for over ten years... at which time I began to toy with flyfishing as something to try when nothing else worked.

Today, my philosophy of flyfishing has changed significantly. I flyfish from the first Dark of the Moon closest to the last two weeks of May or the first two weeks in June until the hatches have ceased in the Fall. Why these precise times? Well, they are generally about the time the Spring Mackinaw action has ceased and the hatches are in abundance.

My old equipment and methods have long since gone by the wayside. And fortunately enough, my equipment is a balanced combination of rod, reel, line, and leader which means efficiency. My success ratio has also improved, currently I hold four world record line classes for trout as recorded in the National Fresh Water Fishing Hall of Fame annals. The following text will explain how the use of proper flyfishing equipment will make a novice flyfisherperson into a moderately successful trout collector from the start.

The Rod

Flyrods generally come in three compositions: glass, graphite, or bamboo. The bamboo rod is the least available item on the market due to its current extreme cost and lack of quality producers. On the other hand, the market is flooded with glass or glass/graphite composition rods which are extremely cheap and have wide fluctuations in quality and durability. The pure graphite flyrod has the quality of extreme sensitivity and is a power rod, their only downfall is the moderately high cost of these units.

For the beginner, I recommend that you choose a glass/graphite composition rod (usually composed primarily of glass with some graphite in the mix). The advantages to this type of rod is one that will fit into almost anyone's budget and they are durable. The moderately advanced to advanced flyfisherperson will be happiest with a one hundred percent graphite rod or a very expensive hand made bamboo rod. I personally use aneight and one-half foot, one hundred percent graphite rod which is moderately priced (under $250.00) and is my pride and joy.

I recommend that you first choose your price range and then decide on the composition of your rod (glass, graphite, etc.). Once this decision is made it is time to analyze those rods to assure you get the best available. I suggest that you forget brand names for now and look for the following quality features.

A. Choose a rod which has many guides throughout its length. A rod with few guides allow the line to slap against the rod and discourage casting.

B. Check that the reel seat will accommodate your reel or select your reel first and make sure it fits the receiver end where reels are attached.

C. Most modern day flyrods have imprinted on the rod a number that corresponds to the size of line which should be used for the rod you are about to purchase.

D. Flyrod lengths are as variable as the lines and leaders that go with them, thus, choose a flyrod which fills balanced when held in your hand. Disregard a friend who insists that only one specific length will do for you.

E. You will notice that most flyrods come in two or more sections and that these sections have either ferrules for joining sections or plugged sections of hollow core which join sections together. The type of ferrule or manner in which they join does not really matter, what matters is that at each joint the two rod pieces do not rotate and fit snugly. I personally prefer a single composition rod in which ferrules are not used . . . using this type of rig adds to the sensitivity of the entire unit.

Most of the specialty fly stores have mentioned to me that customers who are short tend to purchase longer rods than those who are tall. You may not fit into this mold but still choose your own rod.

The Reel

Fly reels generally have but one function, which is to hold line on a spool. These reels seem simple but are as complicated and diverse as any other type of reel. For instance, my choice in a fly reel would be to choose a single action reel with a click drag, a revolving rim (for finger tip drag control) and a spool capacity that will allow about fifty yards of backing with the convenience of extra spools which can be quickly interchanged.

When purchasing a new fly reel you will find that your initial choice will be to purchase either an automatic reel or a single action fly reel. The disadvantage of automatic reels is that they do not generally have the capacity for dacron backing or much leader space and the fact that you will eventually grow out of them. The advantage of this type of reel is that it will quickly zing in your line by simply pressing a lever. The single action reel has a base, spool, and spool crank. It is usually larger and lighter than an automatic and has some type of drag built into the spool. For the beginner, I would recommend a moderately priced reel which contains all of these features and is made in the U.S.A. by one of the larger manufacturers which has convenient warranty centers throughout the Rocky Mountains.

The Line

Now that I have my rod and reel in hand, it should be easy to choose the proper line by just looking at the rod and reading the recommended line to use. This method really helps one to choose the proper weight of line but does not tell you what line to use. For instance, should you use a floating, sinking, or floating/sinking fly line and in a double taper, level, weight forward or shooting taper configuration.

First, lets define our choices relating to line function:

A. Floating fly line floats upon the surface of the water.

B. Sinking fly line sinks slowly toward the river/lake bottom.

C. Floating/Sinking fly line is one which floats for a few seconds and then begins to slowly sink toward the subsurface.

Now, lets define line type.

A. Double Taper (DT) lines have a long level consistent section in the middle and are tapered at each end. When the line begins to wear, simply reverse it.

B. Level (L) lines are of a consistent diameter throughout its length.

C. Weight Forward (WF) lines are weighted on the terminal end, so that more distance can be achieved in casting.

D. Shooting Taper (ST) lines are somewhat unique and specialized, in that, they are attached to a monofilament backing and can be casted long distances.

E. You might note that there are other line types, such as Saltwater Tapers and Bass Bug Tapers. But for our purposes, we will consider only A through D.

Probably the best choice for the beginner and a moderately experienced flyfisherperson is the floating line. It is really a fine all around line for trout, in that, it is permanently buoyant and excels in its presentation of dry flies, wet flies, and streamers fished near the surface. Sinking lines can be successfully used when nymphing, while the floating/sinking lines can be used for both techniques (but you loose a little of the best features of a purely floating or sinking line). I use all three depending on the type of trout fishing I am planning and the water I am going to fish.

The Leader

Choosing the proper leader to attach to your fly line is also a problem. In most flyfishing circles, it is not proper to simply purchase a small spool of level six pound test leader because fly tippet leaders are labeled in terms of diameter not pound test. Thus, you must know by some means a way to convert tippet size into a corresponding line breaking strength. Tippet material generally come in spools designated as level line or tapered leaders. These leaders are marked in line diameter (.011 = 0X) and not by pound test. Pound test can be computed if you: (1) use the same brand of tippet; (2) write the manufacturer and request a line diameter chart which converts their line into pound test; and lastly have a knowledge of industry standard tippet sizes and corresponding diameters (See chart below) which will convert into specific line test categories.

0X = .011″
1X = .010″
2X = .009″
3X = .008″
4X = .007″
5X = .006″
6X = .005″
7X = .004″
8X = .003″

As an example, you may write Berkley and request to know what diameter their 4, 6, and 8 pound test line is for Trilene XL. Once these figures are obtained, just convert to the proper tippet size and now you can go out and purchase the proper tippet in terms of 4X, 5X, 6X, etc. if it is Berkley tippet material you buy.

Additionally, the tippet material manufacturers are aware of the many fledgling fly fishermen about and often label their leaders by first stating the size tippet, then its diameter, and lastly the actual pound test of the line. This solves a lot of computation problems.

I prefer to use a tapered leader of about nine feet in length which has an end breaking strength of about six pound test. Tapered leaders are interesting, in that, they begin at the conjunction of fly line and tippet with an unusually large diameter (.020-.021) and scale down in diameter throughout the entire length until the last eighteen to twenty inches determines the tippet size or final pound test. For instance, a 5X tippet would have a diameter of .006". Tippet diameter is the same for the first eighteen to twenty inches and so is the pound test — but beyond this point, the diameter increases (with the pound test) until only the largest of flies will even accommodate the line diameter.

One last note about leaders. Tippet size corresponds to hook size as follows:

Diameter	Hook Size
0X =	1/0 to 2
1X =	4 to 8
2X =	6 to 10
3X =	10 to 14
4X =	12 to 16
5X =	14 to 20
6X =	16 to 24
7X =	18 to 28
8X =	18 to smallest available

By understanding these concepts, it will be an easy process to purchase a total balanced unit, from the rod, reel, line, leader, to the fly hook size which is best for your usage and a balanced outfit.

The Conjunction

Now that you have a fully balanced rig, you need only one additional bit of information to get you ready for the water. There is one knot that is imperative to know — the Nail Knot. This knot ties the heavy fly line to the monofilament leader. A blow by blow description of how to tie this knot is in the chapter on Knots. Another tip, which deviates from a pure hand tied knot is to use a small plastic cylinder which has holes in both ends and one in the middle. Simply push your fly line through one of the end holes to the common middle hole and tie an overhand knot, trim, and pull. Then repeat this process for the monofilament but double the overhand knot. Wright & McGill (Eagle Claw) is the manufacturer of this particular product. I believe it is the second best connector after the manual Nail Knot.

Flies

There are many types of flies which are used to catch trout and salmon. These flies all fit into the category of dry, wet, streamer, or nymph. They are further defined as follows:

Dry Flies —These flies imitate adult forms of insects that land on the water surface, thus, they are fished directly on the surface. Examples include the Adams, Cahill, or Humpy which imitate the mayflies, cadisses, and midges.

Wet Flies —These flies resemble drowned insects, bait fish, or insects just hatching. They are fished just below the surface. An example of this type of fly is the Black Gnat with a red feather tail.

Nymphs — These flies imitate underwater larvae of insects and are fished below the surface near or on the bottom. An example of this type of insect is the Stonefly, Mayfly larvae, or Midge pupae.

Streamers —These flies imitate bait fish, mice, or large moths and can be fished both on the surface and subsurface. Surface streamers are my personal favorite in lakes, while subsurface streamers generally produce best in the fast flowing river systems of the Rocky Mountains. One of the better surface streamers is the non-weighted Silver Zonker or Black Wooley Worm both tied onto a long shanked size six hook. A great subsurface Rocky Mountain favorite is the Purple Wooley Bugger tied on the same shank as above, this weighted streamer imitates a leach.

I have often been asked the question of which knot to use when attaching a fly to leader material. The knots of choice (which are carefully illustrated in the Knots chapter) are the trilene knot and the improved clench knot. Many other knots are used but these are by far the quickest and easiest to tie.

Casting Methods

It is quite an experience to watch an expert fly fisherperson cast a fly line Twenty to forty yards onto the surface of a lake or river and to wonder how they are able to cast such great distances. You can too, if you follow some simple but necessary procedures consistently.

A. **Grasp your rod as if you were handling a pistol, that is, your fingers should be in front of the reel and your thumb on the top of the rod, as if grasping for the pistol hammer. Your thumb should be pointing toward the rod tip.**

B. **Pull out twenty or thirty feet of line, either coil it at your feet or hold it in comfortable circles in your non-casting hand. Briskly pull the fly rod directly over your shoulder and stop at the eleven o'clock position, allowing the rod to bend backwards until it reaches the one o'clock position, then with your wrist, bring the rod forward at the conclusion of the backward movement, and allow the line to whip forward with gusto until the eleven o'clock position is visualized — then stop your wrist movement abruptly. Your line will smoothly cast through the guides and onto your target.**

The best practice field is a football field because of the yardage markers. I recommend you don't make your goals too lofty at first in terms of casting ability. Try to first become proficient at ten yards and work toward a goal of fifteen yards or forty five feet.

Retrieval Methods

There are many different techniques related to retrieving flies. But until you develop your own technique, probably the most productive of these methods is to simply reach out and pull two or three feet of your line smoothly toward your awaiting forefinger and thumb (that is, if your right handed, your left hand mends the line to your right hand), continue in this manner until you are ready for another cast.

In streams, it is necessary to fish directly above the ripples and allow the fly to float naturally through the ripples and settle into pockets where the fish are concentrated. Any momentary pause of the fly probably indicates a strike, so strike accordingly. As you continue to experiment with your retrieve, you will develop your own effective slow and fast retrieves.

Tricks of the Trade

There are some nifty tricks that you can do with a fly rod, reel, and line that just cannot be done with other outfits. For instance, have you ever fished within a river where a great ripple and subsequent pool existed but you just could not cast because of the foliage? Next time this happens, pull out your fly line and float it down this ripple, disregarding any kind of cast, then spin your rod in a circular motion upstream. You will find that the fly line is lifted off the surface and can be accurately cast upriver in this manner. The line is actually spiraled upriver in a controlled manner and exactly where you want it.

Nymphing

This technique requires the user to attach a significant amount of monofilament to the fly reel, in place of the leader. It is not a traditional nymphing technique but is extremely effective when using a Zonker, size six or a Purple Wooley Bugger. The method is described as follows.

Attach a couple of small split shots to your leader within eighteen inches of your fly. Then read the water, both with your eyes and your head. With a good pair of quality sun glasses, you should be able to recognize fish holding below boulders and in shallow ripples. Cast to the fish. Once your fly has passed, recast, it is unlikely these trout will leave their holding spots to capture your bait. If the fish cannot be spotted, then fish in water where ripples cascade into boulders, undercut banks, or near downed trees and watch your line for the slightest stop, twitch, or a quick sinking motion . . . this is your strike. Several strike indicators are now on the market for the flyfisherman to quickly attach to their leaders, their purpose is to provide a visual of the line suddenly dipping and indicating a strike.

Casting is simple, simply pull out line and cast above the holding area, then allow the line and fly to cascade past your target area in as natural a motion as possible keeping all tension out of the line but also being able to respond to a strike.

Fishing this technique is extremely productive and very effective for the beginner and expert flyfisherman as well because most trout are caught within ten feet of most river banks and casting techniques need not be perfected. Also, this method will creel more large spawning Spring rainbows or Fall spawningbrowns within the confines of most large reservoirs or lake systems primarily near inlets or bays where spawning activity takes place.

July Browns and Rainbows falling for Weighted Purple Wooley Buggers in swift inlet waters.

Springtime Cutthroats from Spiney Reservoir in Colorado, a Flies and Lures only Lake.

Chapter 5

Artificial Lures

Rocky Mountain trout have seen quite an array of spinners, spoons, and plugs for the last several decades. These very effective traditional lures are being challenged by new state-of-the-art artificials developed only in the last few years. This chapter will begin by describing the use of the more traditional artificials, then transcending into the newest array of artificials, and end with some interesting techniques on trolling.

Spinners

One of the most traditional and effective trout artificials is the spinner. All spinners have some basic commonalities such as a blade which rotates around a shaft and a weight underneath for castability. At first glance, they all appear to be pretty much the same except for some streamer material or variations in the weight below (sometimes above) the spinner. I have often wondered why some spinners attract trout better than others.

Two of the most well known trout spinners are the Mepps and the Panther Martin. A close look at these spinners will disclose some very real differences. For instance, the Panther Martin has a blade which is attached directly through the shaft and upon close inspection you will note that the blade is convex on both ends

— this is a sonic blade. The Mepps Spinner has a blade which is attached to the shaft by the use of a clevis which rotates around the shaft.

Is there really a difference in their usage? Yes! The patented sonic blade, because of its design, rotates at a high speed quickly with only the action of a strong current while the Mepps patented blade produces high water resistance in strong currents. Thus, the river fisherman who fishes a deep fast current is probably better off to fish with a spinner which has a sonic blade, whereas, the river fisherman who fishes shallow ripples above pools have an advantage when using a spinner with a clevis.

Another way to look at this is that the Mepps Spinner, because of its higher water resistance has some very real advantages upon its retrieve. Cast at a 45° angle upstream, then apply pressure by taking up the slack, immediately you will feel the action of the blade. There is a tendency for the clevis type attached blade to lift up off the bottom, thus, its use in shallow rapids will mean less snags and more hookups with fish. Using spinners with sonic type blades in fast deep currents where undercut banks are present will net you many large trout. The sonic spinners will penetrate deeper into these depths and rotate extremely fast.

Spinners are clearly the lure of choice in river systems but are they effective in lakes? Spinners used at inlet areas, where water currents are present are excellent. The only negative to fishing lakes with spinners is their light weight . . . these lures are just plain difficult to cast any distance.

The use of a ball bearing swivel is of paramount importance when using spinners to avoid line twist.

Spoons

Spoons were designed for casting distance and primarily for lake application, although some types work well in streams. Most trout fishermen have a wide variety of spoons.

Fishing with spoons seems simple, you put them on, throw them out, and reel them in. It is really not that simple though if you are to match the water to the spoon, that is, what type of spoon is appropriate to the various water conditions?

Most trout fishermen have a wide variety of spoons. They were designed for casting distances primarily in lakes, although some types work well in streams too. Very small spoons are excellent for boat trolling. Upon close examination of your spoons, you will find them in a variety of thicknesses with some variations in design.

Heavy spoons such as Kastmasters allow the user to cast far out into the lake channels where the spoon will sink rapidly and appear as if it is a wounded bait fish or a small fish fleeing from deeper to shallower water.

Spoons of medium thicknesses, such as hammered brass spoons, provide castability into shallow bays where channels crisscross and depths vary. A spoon of this type when retrieved will skitter only a foot or two under the surface. Additionally, it can be quickly skittered across the surface when obvious snags or heavy moss gets in the way. I was once using a hammered brass spoon in a shallow lake full of moss and large trout. By casting out as far as I could, I found that if I reeled like crazy, just after the spoon hit the surface, it would actually plane upon the top of the water until I slowed it to bring it through the deep pockets in the moss. Interestingly enough, the strikes came as the lure passed through these pockets or while being planed across the surface. One seven pound fourteen ounce rainbow actually came from many yards away chasing my lure with his back out of the water all the while.

Spoons of small diameter, such as the Super Duper or Z-Ray typically are designed to imitate wounded bait fish or live minnows, thus, you will find more diversity of design in the small light spoons. Spoons of this type work well in rivers, beaver ponds, small lakes, and the shallow bays and inlets of large impoundments. Castability is sometimes a problem, so you must be sure that the area you choose to fish a light spoon will provide you the opportunity to cast to the mid-point in these areas. Light spoons stay just under the surface and generally have great action.

Extremely light spoons, usually less than one and one half inches, are dynamite for trollers. Use no pop gear but attach the spoon to either your monofilament (which has a small removable shot approximately three feet above) or to a traditional trolling rig with leaded line and a ten to twelve foot monofilament leader. Troll extremely slow and your success will be measured in many strikes. Examples of lures for this application are Dick Nites and Hot Shots. *Be sure to use a ball bearing swivel with all the spoons to avoid line twist.

Minnow Plugs

Minnow plugs generally are made out of two materials, either balsa wood or light weight plastic. These types of lures imitate live minnows and have an action that is difficult to discern from the real thing. The most effective trout plug designs are the floating, sinking, and count down plugs.

An example of a floating plug is the Rainbow Trout Rebel which is jointed to enhance the action. The floating plug, once cast, rests upon the surface until you begin your retrieve, at which time, it dives just under the surface throughout the rest of your retrieve. This type of lure is best used in shallow bays or rivers where snags or heavy weed beds are the rule. Spring and Fall spawning trout are a sure bet to latch on to one of these lures as they make their way into the shallow bays and inlets of most impoundments.

The sinking plug, in which you can purchase both jointed and unjointed floats upon the surface until you begin your retrieve and then begins to dive several feet under the surface. The Sinking Rapala is an excellent choice to use in areas which are full of below water shelves that give way to channels. This type of plug is generally used in large deep lakes and reservoirs.

The count down plug is really remarkable. It is the closest thing to having your own personal electronic depth finder. A count down plug sinks at about the rate of one foot per second and will continue to sink until you begin your retrieve. Once the retrieve has begun this lure will maintain its depth. For example, cast out a count down lure as far as you can, once it hits the water, count from one to ten, then reel in smoothly (you will be at an approximate depth of ten feet). If no strike occurs in two or three casts, then on the next cast count down from one to twelve, then fourteen, sixteen, etc. When you get a strike, say at twelve, you will know where the trout are suspended . . . and if you land this fish and it happens to be a rainbow, you will further know (because of Chapter 1) that the ideal feeding water temperature for rainbow trout is 55°F, thus, browns will be caught in warmer water, say at a countdown of ten, and brook trout will be caught just below this level probably at thirteen (the ideal feeding water temperature of brook trout is 54°F. Once you locate fish, you can move throughout the lake and catch the species you seek just by using this count down method. *Never use a swivel on minnow plugs, it impedes the lures natural action.

Soft-bodied Lures

Bass fishermen for decades have been keenly aware of the benefits of using a vast variety of soft rubbery artificial lures. Most trout fisherman's tackle boxes contain no soft rubbery artificials and corresponding lead head jigs of any type. It has been only in the past couple of years that Western trout fishermen have begun to experiment with them. I have personally caught trout in the State of Colorado in excess of thirty two pounds by the use of these types of artificials and perhaps started a myriad of experimentation with them.

For years, fishermen have asked me what I use to catch these big fish . . . my answer was not exactly on the money, but close. I made statements like, 'Use Mister Twister with a 1/4 oz. round jig head'. I did not state the color, the exact lure, the technique, nor that I always tip my jigs with whole two to three inch suckers or when using the smaller 1/16 or 1/32 oz. jigs I typically tip them with Eurolarvae.

The method that I am about to describe will net you more large trout than any other method that I know of and it is usable year round. I will begin with the large soft plastic lures and corresponding jig heads then make a transition into the use of the small soft plastics. But first, it is important to note that while these methods can be used year round, for all practical purposes, if you do not have a boat, these methods are for ice fishing. I fish them year round and can assure that if you closely follow this method for success, a fifteen pound Winter or Summer trout is right in the ballpark.

First, you need the proper equipment which includes one three foot (cheap $5.00 to $6.00) glass rod with a cork handle and two sliding rings to hold your reel; a large open faced bail reel, and twelve pound Berkley Trilene XT on your reel spool. Attach to the line a good quality ball bearing swivel, a white quarter ounce jig head and lastly the secret that I have kept quiet for the last decade — a white Sassy Shad, white or smoke sparkle soft plastic squid like skirts, and a two to three inch whole frozen sucker. The soft plastic squid or hula skirts go over the Sassy Shad to create an all soft lure which looks like nothing alive that I have ever seen before. Mackinaw and brown trout go bonkers over this rig.

The Method

Auger an ice hole of at least ten inches in diameter or two overlapping seven to eight inch holes (the fish you catch may not fit through the holes if you don't). Note that a ball bearing swivel is used when fishing through the ice and is not used when fishing open water. Generally a swivel should not be used on jigs but because of water density in winter and this particular jigging action it is necessary to use one. *Note that I recommend you select only swivels that are black in color (stainless or brass colors sometimes attract the fish to strike the swivel).

Method A: Using a 1/4 oz. Jig or Larger

Allow your jig to cascade down through the depths and onto the bottom. At this time, take up the slack and begin a slow steady thumping pumping action, once the jig is two feet off of the bottom allow it to quickly sink to the bottom again, and continue this action. A strike will be felt only as a pressure on the rod or a slight jerk. Set the rod hard (my 32½ pounder hit like a 6 inch trout) and hold on.

Rocky Mountain Mackinaw often weigh in excess of twenty pounds. This one weighed thirty two pounds and resides on my wall.

You might be curious how a pressure strike can be felt. One of the main reasons, besides their durability, to purchase a short glass rod with sliding rings is to be able to exactly balance the rod to the reel. Once balanced you will note when holding the rod/reel combination in the jigging position that it sets exactly horizontal to the ice cover or the open water and is balanced, by itself, on your first two fingers. Thus, once my jig has hit bottom, I simply use my thumb to tap the butt while slowly raising the rod the rod (and the jig off of the bottom) to the maximum two foot level. This action creates a slowly fluttering active jig.

Method B: Using a 1/16 oz. or Smaller Jig

Select a jig, preferably one that offers the user colors that glow in the dark, and that are tied with chenille bodies. Rig as previously described except tip this jig with corn grubs, meal worms, or Eurolarvae. Then, if you can, beg, borrow, purchase, or convert your own favorite sonar unit into a portable unit. Once this is done, seek previously productive waters that are fifty eight to sixty two feet deep with structure. Once this is achieved, turn up your gain and search for the zoo plankton layer (seen as dots or a solid line and usually twenty to thirty five feet deep).

** Note that many ice fishermen are under the impression that this is a thermocline layer of water present year round. But not so, the thermocline layer of water does not exist in Rocky Mountain Lakes at this time of year because they are too cold. You are observing zoo plankton, a living phenomena which is usually only visible in large impoundments which have a significant underwater vegetation. In smaller more sterile waters where vegetation exists but not to this degree, this layer can be found by pinpointing suspended concentrations of fish.

Once this layer of living matter is found or concentrations of suspended fish, simply lower your jig, watch your screen, and fish within its confines. Jig in the same manner as described in A, But your imaginary bottom is the plankton layer or suspended fish. When fishing in this layer use two small jig rods and alternate between them, jigging one and a few minutes later, the other. You will often find the rainbows, cutthroats, and brown trout will hit the jig which is not moving but within their feeding layer.

Additional tips to consider. Many ice fishermen prefer to use wire tips on their poles to detect the slightest strike. A tip of this type is useful when fishing suspended or bottom baits, but I have personally had problems with them tangling the line or bending straight when fighting a large trout. I recommend that you try a strike indicator (such as a styrofoam peanut) which allows you to see the slightest strike and upon setting the hook it disintegrates, thus, no breakage or fouled line.

Trolling Tips

Trolling seems pretty simple . . . just crank up the boat engine, throw out the bait, and motor around until you get a bite. You might be surprised at the new state-of-the-art techniques that have impacted this type of fishing.

Side planers are now being developed that allow your line and bait to literally plane along side your boat as far away as you wish. The advantage is that the boat propeller disruption upon the water does not even cross your trolled presentation. A real plus!

And downriggers have become efficient to the point that computer chips have even been incorporated into units to gauge depth and allow the downrigger to rise when humps or large boulders are about to be trolled into or they lower when a large depression on the bottom is noted. The only snag you could catch with this unit would be large trout. These units are very expensive now, but as time goes on, and competition impacts these units, the price will fall.

Trolling lures range from spoons, attractor blades to be used with bait or small spoons, and deep diving plugs. Spoons must be attached directly to a swivel and then to the monofilament line to avoid line twist while trolling. Most attractor blades utilize a two to three foot leader with a small lure or bait attached to a single hook. Deep diving plugs are a favorite to use with downriggers or when attached directly to monofilament and slowly trolled just under the surface.

I have used a method over the years that has been extremely successful and has added a new dimension to my trolling skills. Use a level wind reel filled with lead core line, attach a ball bearing swivel, add twelve to twenty feet of monofilament, and attach a small lure or night crawler. Pay out the line and use the slowest trolling speed available.

If you need more depth, attach a single sliding sinker to the lead core line before the swivel. The theory is that the lead core line actually trolls deeper than the monofilament leader which rises above the leaded line and appears to the fish not to be associated with the very visible leaded line. The longer the leader, the higher the presentation.

Chapter 6

Knots and Rigging

The weakest link in any system could destroy the most sophisticated system of all. This is usually relevant when you have purchased a complete fishing system (e.g., rod, reel, line, and tackle). The best system is comparable to the worst if proper care is not given to the choice of knots and rigging to use. This chapter is designed to make you familiar with a number of knots, their purpose, and how they build upon one another to make a rig.

1. The Slip Cinch

Purpose: To join a spool of new line to your reel spool.

Benefit: The line once cinched up will not slip, thus will not twist as line is spooled on. Additionally, this knot can easily be removed without cutting by simply taking the tip of a hook and placing it under the first coil, then pull. It slips off as easily as it slipped on and the benefit is no spool damage from cutting this cinch loop with a knife.

A.

Spool

Tie a slip knot first, then tie an overhand knot on the terminal end of the line

B.

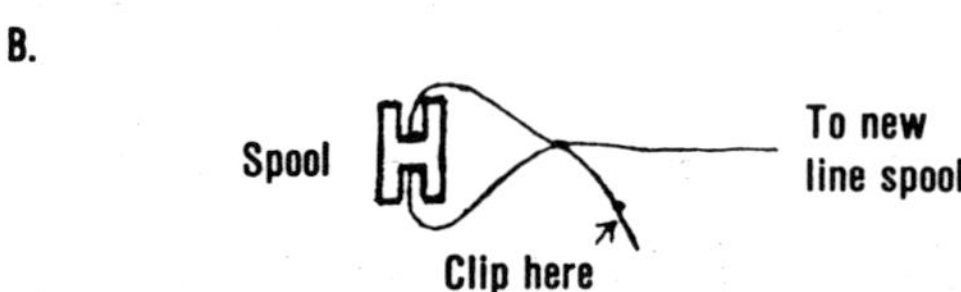

Put slip knot over spool, clip this end outside of the reel, pull tight and you are ready to reel on your new line.

2. The Professionally Hand Snelled Hook

Purpose: To assure a quality snell for loose hooks and to teach you the first step in tying the Leeper Keeper Adjusta Hook.

Benefit: Allows the maker to purchase quality loose hooks and to snell cheaper than they can be purchased on the open market. Also, purchased snelled hooks are generally machine snelled where lines overlap or are poorly snelled.

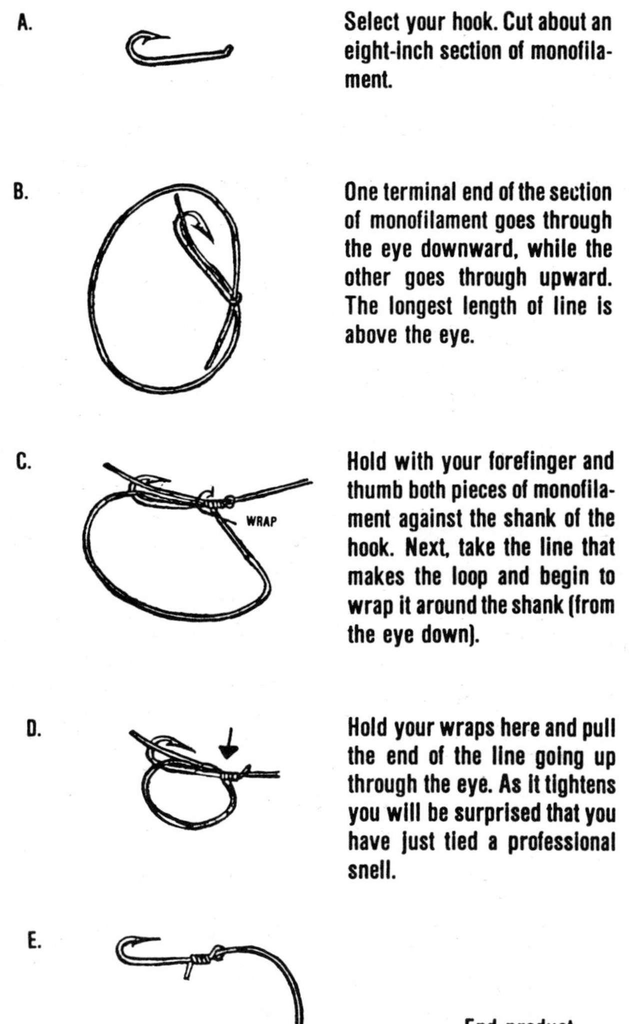

3. The Trilene Knot

Purpose: To attach swivels, hooks, and lures to a knot which is almost as strong as the line test and secures the tackle with two loops (see illustration).

Benefit: The conjunction of choice when attaching monofilament to various components of tackle and a necessary conjunction when tying the Adjusta Hook rig or when attaching large streamer flies to a leader.

A.

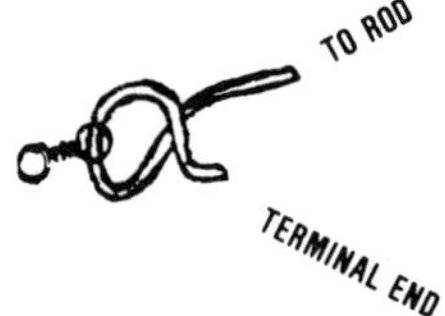

Take line through swivel to form a loop.

B.

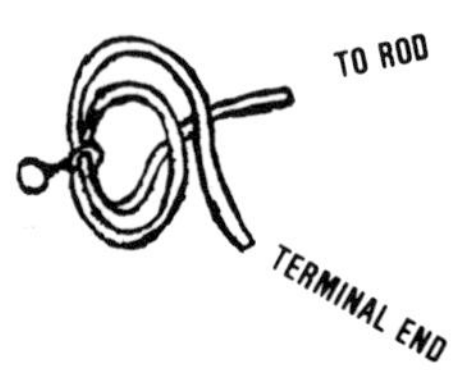

Repeat step A so that your line has gone through the swivel twice.

C.

You then wrap the terminal end of the line around your line going to the rod tip (about four times). Note loops A & B.

D.

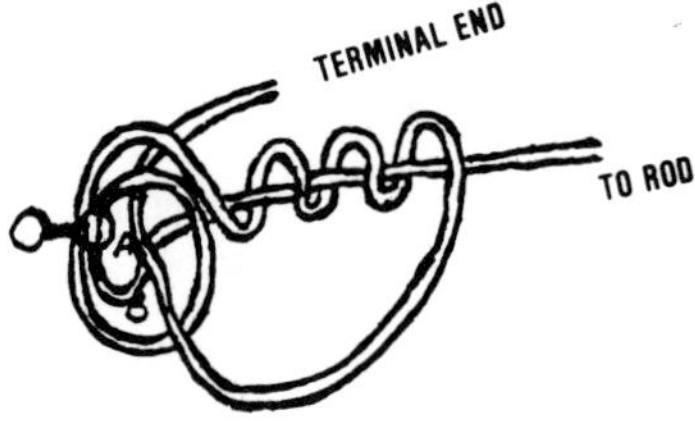

Take the terminal end of your line and put it through loops A & B.

E.

Cinch down by pulling both the terminal end and the line to your rod tip.

I personally prefer the trilene knot, since the monofilament actually grasps the eyelet of the hook with two strands of mono (A & B) instead of one.

4. The Leeper Keeper Adjusta Hook

Purpose: To accomodate any size whole bait or cut filet. First hook is professionally snelled while the second hook is also professionally snelled upon the main line, thus, this second hook slides free upon the line.

Benefit: Allows a great natural presentation when using whole bait (head first presentation).

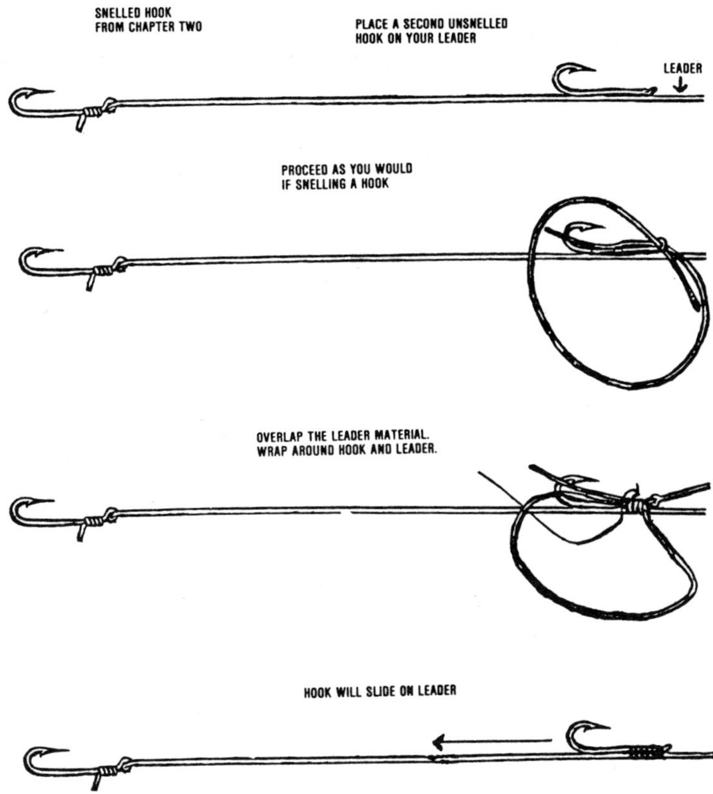

5. The Blood Knot

Purpose: To join two lines of the same diameter together. Such as eight pound test to eight pound test.

Benefit: Is nearly as strong a conjunction as the line itself. Good for leader attachments or adding line to a reel that is far into the backing.

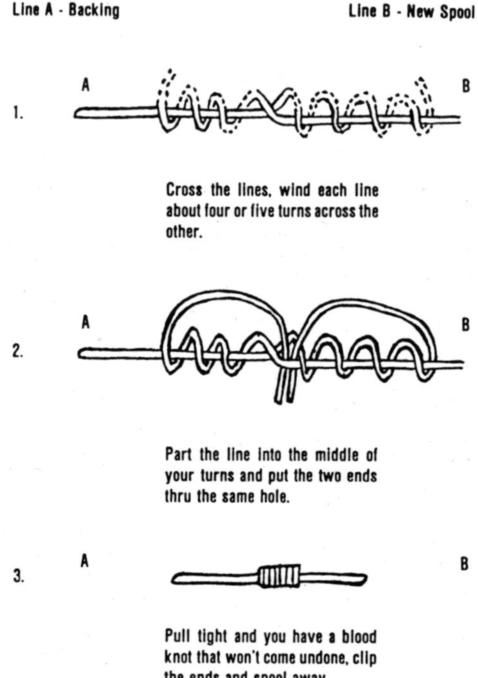

6. The Blood Dropper

Purpose: To place upon a segment of monofilament line round droppers (circular conjunctions) which will receive snelled hooks or snelled flies.

Benefit: Droppers stay rigid away from your line and allow attachment of bait hooks, flies, or lures. No better continuous leader from your reel spool to the end of your line is more natural than tying these droppers . . . use this setup for use with a spinning rod, fly, and bubble or as a second fly dropper when using conventional fly equipment.

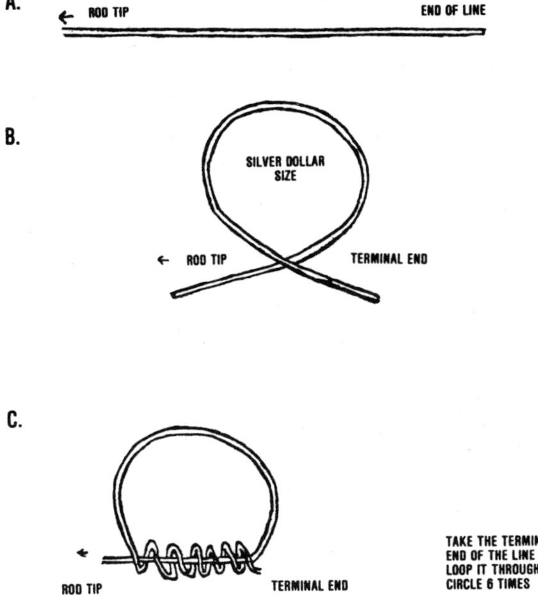

D.

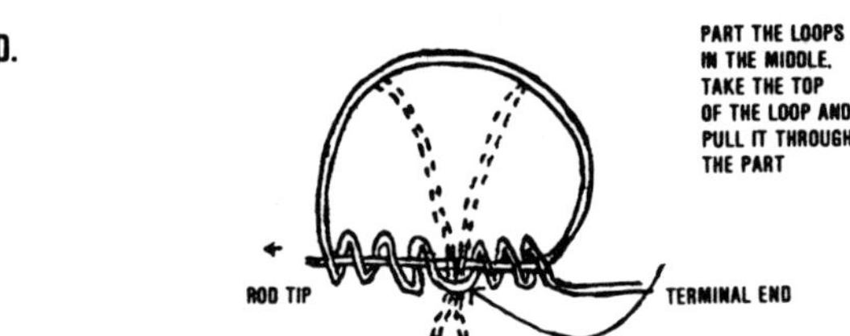
PART THE LOOPS
IN THE MIDDLE.
TAKE THE TOP
OF THE LOOP AND
PULL IT THROUGH
THE PART
ROD TIP
TERMINAL END

E.

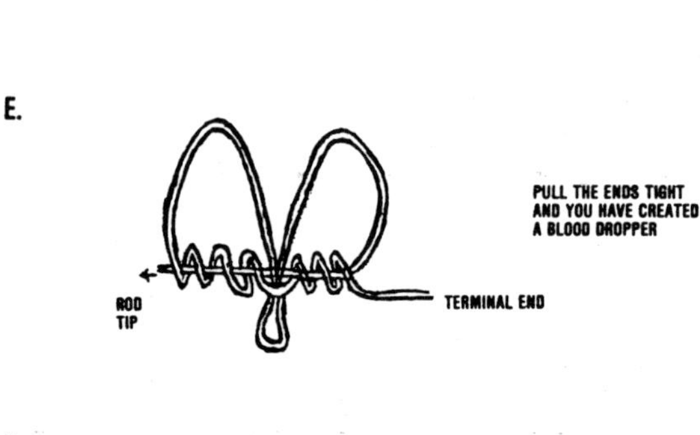
PULL THE ENDS TIGHT
AND YOU HAVE CREATED
A BLOOD DROPPER
ROD
TIP
TERMINAL END

F.

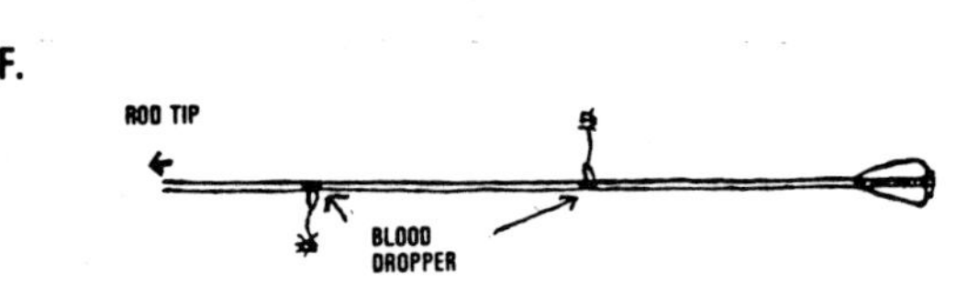
ROD TIP
BLOOD
DROPPER

7. The Nail Knot

Purpose: To join two lines of different diameters together such as a fly line to a tapered leader or level leader.

Benefit: This knot will not slip and is the knot of choice when used in flyfishing applications.

A. Place a large needle between your fly line and connecting monofilament.

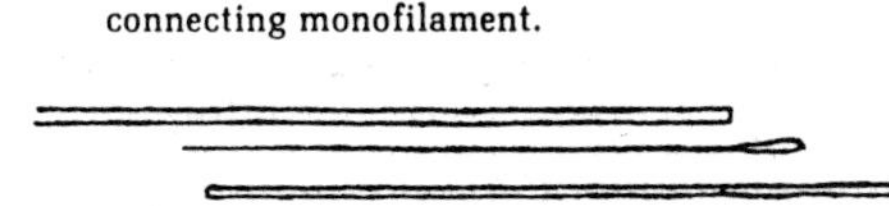

B. Wrap monofilament around fly line and needle.

C. Thread needle with the monofilament as shown.

D. Pull needle through and pull the leader tight. The finished product will be neat and strong.

8. Improved Clench Knot

Purpose: To join line to terminal tackle.

Benefit: The knot of choice for years before the advent of the Trilene Knot.

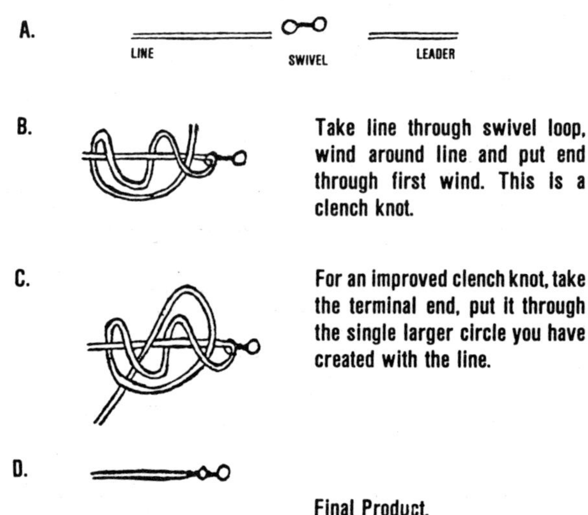

9. Sliding Bubble Rig

The use of floats with bait has always been an excellent method to use when fishing for crappie or blue gill, but is not always as successful when fishing for the deeper suspended cold water fish such as trout. An excellent setup to use to get to these fish is the old sliding bubble trick. Use a bubble, which will allow the line to freewheel through it, attach a three foot leader and a barrel swivel in the following manner. You will be able to cast great distances and present a bait naturally.

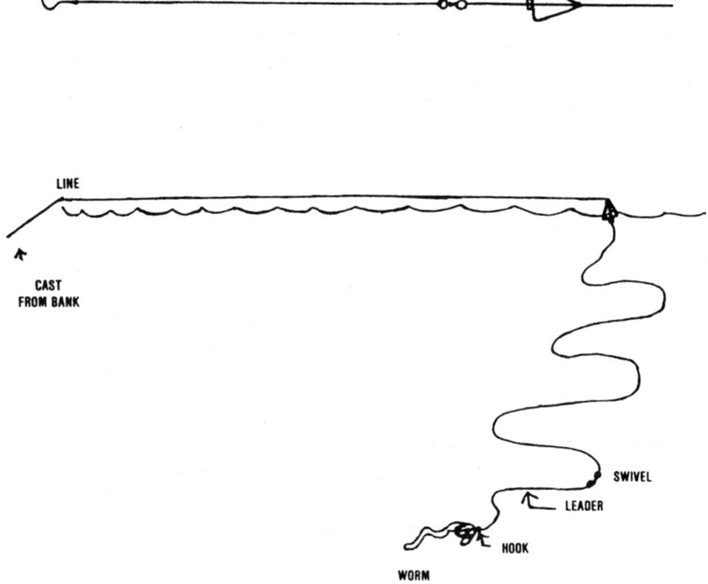

10. Beaded Keel Sinker Rigs

Purpose: This rig is designed to be used with a spinning rod and large streamer flies. The water of the Miracle Mile in Wyoming, the Big Horn in Montana, and the Green River just below Flaming Gorge in Utah has many fast flowing deep water pools which are not fished very heavily because of the difficulty of getting to the fish on the bottom. Benefit: A dynamite method which will allow successful fishing in deep fast flowing pools.

The technique is to attach a beaded keel sinker to a three-foot leader and attach a large fly to the end. Cast upstream at about a forty-five degree angle and allow your line to rapidly drift down river while retrieving just fast enough to keep from hitting the bottom.

11. Fly and Bubble Rig:

Purpose: To be used with a spinning rod.
Benefit: An improved technique for an old effective method which features the bubble at the terminal end of the line.

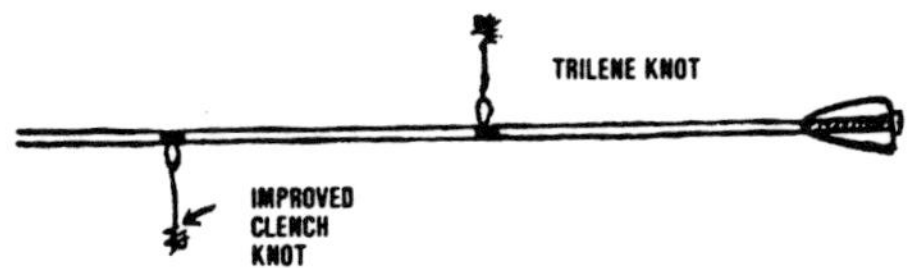

I am sure that you noticed right away that the bubble is at the terminal end of the line. Furthermore, which comes first, the bubble or the flies — in this case the flies. When rigging with the bubble just beyond the rod tip, the fish first see the bubble or water disruption which discourages a lot of strikes by larger fish. This method will creel fifty percent more strikes and larger fish.

The bubble is illustrated below for further investigation. The product is called an Adjusta Bubble and allows line to go through a seated chamber of hollow surgical rubber which when twisted firmly attaches the line at any location on your main line you desire, thus, no knots and there is a chamber which can be opened to allow water to enter for casting weight.

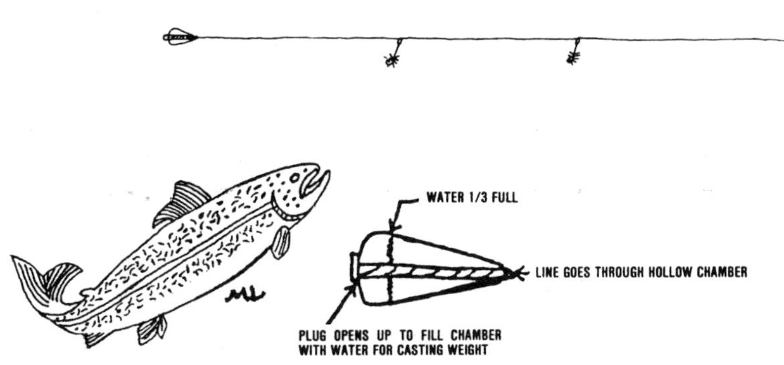

Chapter 7

Equipment

The emphasis of most fishing related books is to totally focus upon the experience, method, or technique of catching fish. This book, thus far, is no exception, until now. Your equipment is the basis of the entire sport and very little information exists on the positives and negatives these products, their best use, and the product of choice among many.

Rods

I have approximately twenty five rods that I am constantly using for a number of fishing applications. Some can be considered to be very specialized, while others are a necessity, in any event, none sit around to gather dust more than a few weeks. The composition of rods will be discussed only briefly because, no single composition is best, it depends entirely upon the time of the year your fishing, whether it is day or night, and weather conditions.

Compositions:

A. Fiberglass:

A quality of fiberglass is that it is extremely durable, flexible, and economical.

B. Graphite Composition:

Rods of this type contain both fiberglass and graphite fibers for strength and maximum flexibility.

C. Graphite:

Graphite composition rods can be thought of as power rods which have the qualities of extreme sensitivity from tip to butt and unusual strength.

D. Boron:

Rods of this type are touted to be stronger and more sensitive than graphite but those that I've used have the feel of a pool cue and are unusually short.

E. Bamboo:

Bamboo rods in the early part of the century were the rods of choice over steel rods of the time. The current popularity of bamboo is primarily limited to their use in the manufacturing of split bamboo fly rods. These rods require yearly maintenance and do not have the power of modern day compositions.

Rod Types:

A. Spinning:

Spinning rods typically have long cork handles, a reel seat which accommodates an open faced reel (below the rod), big guides, and long length (six and one-half to eight feet for Rocky Mountain Usage).

B. Spin-Casting:

Typical spin cast rods are five to six and one-half feet long. They are made to accommodate closed faced reels which fit comfortably in a specially designed reel seat. They usually have a finger trigger for casting ease and large guides which reduces friction when casting.

C. Spinning Trigger Rods:

These rods are typical spinning rods which are longer than the normal Rocky Mountain rods (seven to eight feet), they often are equipped with Fuji guides, and they all have a trigger just below the reel seat. This rod is somewhat of a specialty rod and can be used with salt water squidder reels or large capacity closed faced reels. Rocky Mountain trout fishermen use them as the rod of choice when fishing at night for large trout when closed faced reels and the length between large streamer flies is paramount to success.

D. Trolling Rods:

Trolling rods are generally short heavy rods of various compositions which are used to deep water troll from boats using downriggers or heavy lead core line. These rods are generally used with specialty level wind reels.

E. Fly Rods:

Fly rods are typically long and limber (eight and one-half to twelve feet) power rods which are specifically used in conjunction with specially designed fly line, leader, and reels. This type of outfit is typically used in rivers, streams or beaver ponds where the primary bait used is artificial flies.

You may have noticed that most modern day rods have no metal ferrules which reduce overall sensitivity. Today's rod ferrules are made of fiberglass or graphite and are incorporated into the rod design and the molding process. Additionally, the guides offer the angler two choices, the single foot guide and the traditional double foot guide. A single foot guide offers the angler increased sensitivity throughout the length of the rod. The double foot guide wraps over several more inches of the composition material used and suppresses sensitivity and performance.

Reels:

There are basically only four types of reels used by Rocky Mountain fishermen, they are the spinning (open faced), spin casting (closed faced), fly, and level wind reels. Of these, the simplest to understand and use is the fly and level wind types which are used to coil fly line and troll with heavy lead core line in conjunction with downriggers. The open and closed faced reels have enough unique and novel features that it is necessary to discuss and highlight their best uses and features so that we can both choose and distinguish the better quality products.

Open Faced Reels:

Open faced reels seem to fit one mold only. They have a bail, drags at the front of the spool or rear of the reel, and exposed line which coils off the reel spool with ease and without tangle. What else could we say? Plenty! Do not use the cost of a reel or its brand name to gauge quality, look for these features.

1. Be sure that the bail, in antireverse, has a number of stops every inch or so all around the spool. This feature alone will save you from losing large Mackinaw, brown, or rainbow trout which hit with ferocity and a vengeance of a run away freight train. Note that a large number of open faced reels do not have these stops and must snap back vigorously to the twelve o'clock casting position each time. An aggressive strike will snap your line with a force so sharp that it will severly weaken or cleanly break your best monofilament.

2. I also recommend that you purchase an additional spool which is shallow in nature to allow the use of small diameter lines that will spool only one hundred to one hundred fifty yards of line in the four, six, and eight pound tests. Some reel spools will comfortably carry three hundred yards of twelve pound test line. You can see from this statement that to fill a spool of this type with six pound line you would need about five hundred yards to do so, thus, the shallow spool will be your ticket to using small diameter lines for nymphing or small bait applications.

Closed Faced Reels:

Closed faced reels have a push button mechanism which releases the line and a cap which fully encloses the spool from the elements.

Their design makes casting easier and reduces tangling because of their ease in use. Modern closed faced reels with large capacity spools, star or friction drags, and fast retrieves are comparable feature to feature with the open faced reels. This is the reel of choice when flyfishing at night for big browns because the closed faced reel allows the users to spool the line through their thumb and forefinger just in front of the reel, while the open faced reel requires the user to reach up toward the first guide and hold the line there (which after just a few short minutes makes your back ache unless you are a contortionist). Also a blood dropper is tied just in front of the reel face but is pulled completely closed to make a knot which tells the fisherman he/she is ready to cast again — that is, when this knot is felt, the top fly is only four inches from the rod tip, thus, you don't need to turn on a light at night to see where your flies are so you can cast.

Camping Equipment:

There is very little information on the exact needs of the Rocky Mountain sportsman who fishes and hunts year round. Most advertisements are slanted to sell a particular item and not necessarily the best item for the climate. And often, our age is a determinator of desirable camping needs as our budget and comfort needs grow. I can clearly remember when I was in high school and my only camping needs were a good sleeping bag and tarp. Later after Viet Nam, my needs or desires required me to purchase a camper shell, and now a camper. My next step, probably in retirement, will be either a fifth wheel or a motor home. In any event, it is my goal to discuss these comforts from sleeping on the ground to campers and motor homes and which is best.

Sleeping Bags:

My budget has always dictated the quality of my equipment and when buying my first sleeping bag, it was no different. My first bag was a three pound surplus army bag which needed some patching and the addition of a heavy blanket to keep from freezing even with my clothes on. Now-a-days a tight budget can get you some real quality if you shop carefully and use one of the large mail order companies who specialize in outdoor equipment.

The Rocky Mountain angler should have a sleeping bag of at least five pounds and guaranteed to -30°F. Most bags of this quality are in the two to three hundred dollar range . . . but what if you could get a generic brand of the same quality for only $99. Well, you can and the quality of this product is first class. You can find these items in the catalogues of the following mail order outlets: Cabela's, Gander Mountain, Pro Bass Shops, Eddie Bower Outdoor Outfitters, REI and many more. I prefer a bag which is rectangular in shape and as wide as I can get. This type of bag will keep you warm even if your sleeping on the ground with only a tarp thrown over you to keep the weather out.

Tents:

I have had many successes and failures when purchasing tents over the last forty years. It seems that the small two to three person tents are built for 'Hobbits', I have never seen one yet which could actually accommodate three normal size persons. Thus, I warn you, when purchasing a tent, never but never, purchase one unless it is set up and you have a chance to sit and lay down in it. A five man tent is just about right for my spouse, Mary and myself. That is, there is room for our two sleeping bags, a bit of space to place ice chests, fishing rods, etc. at our feet and on one side and that is it.

I believe your best buy today, again through the mail order houses, is one of the double domed, insulated, with a bottom, Geodesic tents which because of their design keep the cold out and the heat in. The cost range for name brand tents of this type is between $160 and $350 . . . but they are the best available and sure beat the cost of a truck and camper.

Camper Shells:

This might be a great alternative because once a camper shell is installed then the bed of the pickup can be modified to accommodate mattresses, camping stoves, propane lanterns, catalic heaters, etc. and the cost can be kept way down by purchasing one used. Believe it or not, if you have the time to shop around in any large Rocky Mountain Metropolitan Area, you will find a large number of these shells which have been used very little. For $200, you should be able to find one which will fulfill your current needs.

New camper shells cost in the range of $300 to $600 depending upon the brand.

Campers:

Yes, we have all said, "I'll never have one of those big gas guzzling campers on my truck." Age and comfort have a way of changing one's mind, but even I, would not consider this change until the pop-up campers hit the West. Now I could enjoy the benefits of a low profile (almost like a shell) which could be popped up to accommodate a person seven feet tall. The difference in my mileage only changed three miles per gallon, from 16 to 13, not bad considering my rig has a fuel injected 460 V8 as its powerplant and is the largest 4X4 3/4 ton made.

In fact, I can't say more about comfort, warmth, and the reliability of these rigs. On the inside, they look like a small motel room and they are complete with safe vented to the outside propane stoves, thermostatically controlled heaters, refrigerators, two to three beds, stainless steel sinks, cabinets galore, etc. And all for less than the cost of a mountain lot, a good quality snowmobile, or most business computers. Further more, these campers allow the owner to hook up to city water or electricity if a KOA campground or similar facility is nearby for just a few dollars a night.

I call this rig, the over thirty rig, which is just about the time I could stand my shell no longer. As you can see by the photograph (below), my rig is as large as the full sized camper next to it without the weight or wind resistance when down. My rig is called a Sun Lite, I looked hard for this unit and found that it was nearly identical to similar units throughout the Rocky Mountains which were literally over a thousand dollars higher in price.

My Sun Lite is actually larger than the conventional campers parked next to it when up and like a shell when down . . . this equates to gas savings and the ability to four wheel drive into some pretty tight spots.

If your interested in a unit of this type, then I recommend that you contact Rocky Mountain Campers, Inc. of Denver, Colo. at (303) 233-6716. The owner is a fellow fishing and hunting fanatic who will fairly assess your needs and if this rig is for you, will quote a price which sounds like a wholesale price, rather than a retail price.

My reasons for purchasing this unit related to price, availability, warranty, and the fact that Rocky Mountain RV has been around over two decades servicing these units throughout the entire Rocky Mountains.

Fifth Wheel:

Now that I am 46, my eyes are beginning to wander toward a fifth wheel because they offer the convenience of leaving off (easily) the rig on a camp site while I hunt or fish in areas accessible only with my four wheeler. My camper comes off with jacks too, but again, the comfort level in a fifth wheel is comparable to a small two bedroom home. I have often thought that it would be nice to invest in a mountain home close to one of my favorite Rocky Mountain Lakes where I could fish and hunt to my hearts delight. But when I get down to it, that is not where my needs lie, I need the mobility to fish places such as, the Big Horn in the Fall, Flaming Gorge and the Green River in the Spring, and Granby Dam during the Winter months and if I had a mountain home that would be the place of primary interest because of the investment and convenience.

The only drawback I see is the cost. It is comparable to a small home and it depreciates much like a mobile home or motor home. The bar none best buy is to purchase one that is used. There is currently a glut of them on the market with very little mileage on them and discounts which measure many thousands of dollars. So, right now, I'm satisfied with my Sun Lite. I believe that it, or a comparable camper of its type, is the ultimate in Rocky Mountain camping product for durability, cost, and workmanship.

Boots:

One thing that I cannot handle is cold feet. When I was in my early twenties I had a bout with frost bite on my toes which was serious enough to create a life long sensitivity to the cold. Over the years, I have probably tried most of the manufacturers who advertise various claims regarding how warm their boots were. The ones that caught my eye related to boots worn in the Canadian Shield Area — to date, I have three of these pairs of boots that I will never wear out because they sit in my camper gathering dust . . . the reason is that my feet got cold and I stumbled onto a boot which far exceeds stated claims for warmness.

The product is called Mickey Mouse Boots or more accurately 'Boot, Insulated, Cold Weather, Rubber (Black or White) for Wet-Cold Use, Type 1, Class 1, Rigid Sole'. These are military boots developed for the troops in Alaska and have been standard issue to workers on the Alaskan pipeline by the various oil companies. A new friend, Lindsay Mundell, who developed into one of my best and most trusted friends told me about these boots on our first hunting outing. I believed him and called around to find that these boots new cost around $150., but at local surplus stores they could be found used for $60. or new for $75. Thus, I started out with a used White, Size 12, Extra Wide pair. My backup pair are Black and cost $60 too. The benefit is, I have been in weather which has dipped below -35°F and never gotton cold yet. This includes all day ice fishing activities and big game hunting in calf deep snow. Thus, I highly recommend that you consider these boots as an option to cold frostbitten feet. *The boots far exceed the manufacturers claims in that the attached instruction tag indicates that the boots are good only to -20°F.

Depth Finders:

It used to be that only boat fishermen purchased depth finders, now days, it is a common sight to see sophisticated models on shelves in garages awaiting the winter ice cover. This is the time to catch larger trout without the crowds of summer tromping about. The process of locating fish with these units is fairly easy once you understand the functions of your unit. Some units have so many functions that not all are understood and few are used. For instance, it took me several seasons to realize that my unit actually had the capacity to display to me *on the screen* fish swimming up to my bait and hitting it. You may have had this problem too or were not aware of your units total capabilities.

To see fish strike your bait, simply slow down your scroll from 8.0 to 4.0 and turn the gain up all the way. You will be amazed as you see fish rush up from the depths to strike your bait before you see it on your rod.